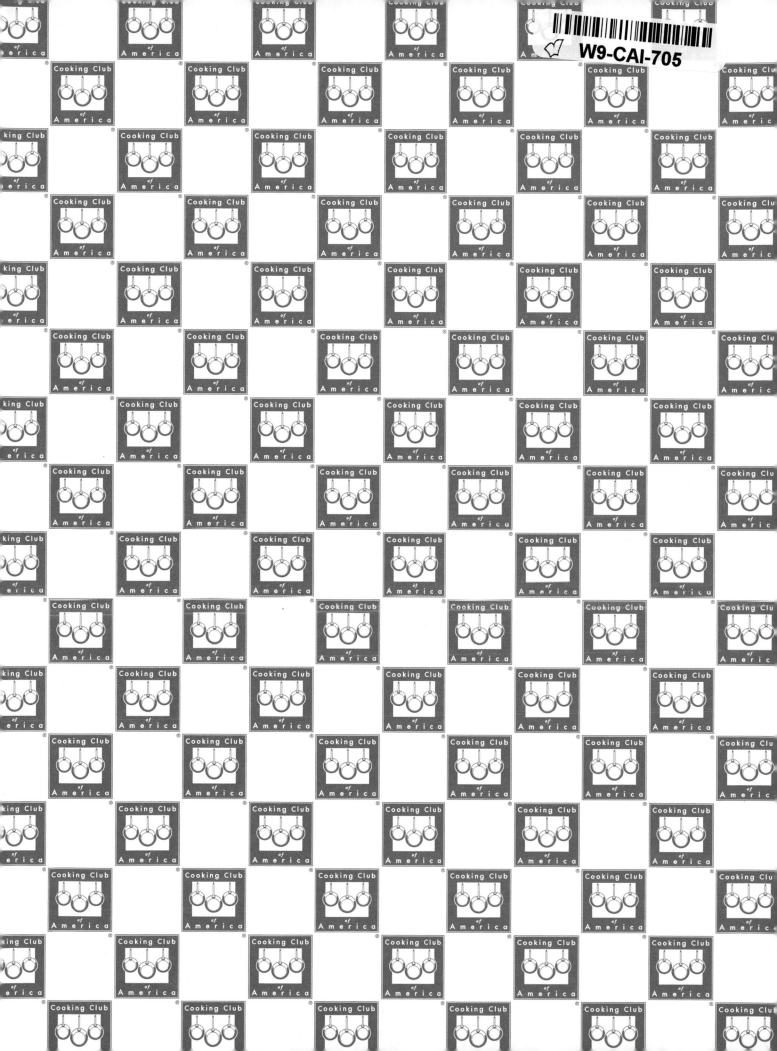

Favorites Around the Table

MEMBER RECIPES

Minnetonka *Minnesota*

Favorites Around the Table—Member Recipes

Tom Carpenter
Director of Book Development

Dan Kennedy
Book Production Manager

Jennifer Guinea
Book Development Coordinator

Zachary Marell
Book Design and Production

Mowers Photography
Commissioned Photography

Mary Lane
Food Stylist

3 4 5 6 7 8 / 05 04 03 02 01

ISBN 1-58159-094-6

Cooking Club of America
12301 Whitewater Drive
Minnetonka, MN 55343
www.cookingclub.com

Contents

Introduction 4

Appetizers & Beverages 5

Breads 17

Soups & Salads 31

Sides 49

Meats 61

Poultry 79

Fish & Seafood 89

Meatless 103

Desserts 115

Bars, Candies & Cookies 135

Index 153

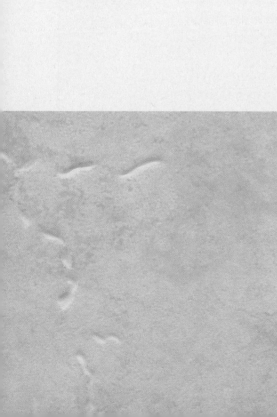

Welcome to *Favorites Around the Table*... and recipes from friends!

There are many places to find a good recipe.

Cookbooks, of course, present dozens and sometimes hundreds of ideas. Magazines like *Cooking Pleasures* and even special newspaper sections bring you more ideas. Think of all the other publications with recipes that cross your countertop in the course of a year. And what about all those recipes you find on product packages? And now, with the internet in so many homes, a world of food awaits on your computer screen ...

These are all great resources. But there's one place where you can get recipe ideas that have a special something extra ... from a friend — someone you know, like and trust.

At the Cooking Club of America, we think one of the best sources for this special kind of recipe is our membership — real people like you who cook a lot, cook well, are open to new ideas and challenges, know what's good, and can really appreciate a great new idea or a special twist on something tried-and-true.

Every member idea in *Favorites Around the Table* is that special kind of recipe because it is the kind you get from a friend: something that has been created many times, adjusted and fine-tuned to perfection by someone who loves food and the people they're creating it for.

So these recipes hold real meaning, and they are among the personal favorites of Cooking Club of America members, your friends. When you make one of these delicious ideas, remember where it came from, that it's not just another recipe rolling through your kitchen. It's something special, and it may have even been in a family for generations.

Some of these recipes are simple and convenient, others are involved and fancy, and many fall somewhere in between. You'll find favorites around the table — from appetizers to main dishes, sides, soups and salads, desserts and more. So each of these 230 dishes is, in one way or another, a work of art — food art — shared between friends. That's the kind of recipes these are, and the kind of cookbook this is. Enjoy!

Appetizers
& Beverages

WONTON CUPS

Lori Ann Kwiatkowski
New Port Richey, Florida

1 (12-oz.) pkg. bulk hot sausage

1 (1-oz.) pkg. powdered ranch salad dressing mix

1 cup mayonnaise

1 cup milk

1½ cups sharp cheddar cheese (6 oz.)

1½ cups Monterey Jack cheese (6 oz.)

½ cup chopped red bell pepper

1 (2¼-oz.) can sliced ripe olives, finely chopped

36 to 40 wonton skins

3 to 4 tablespoons vegetable oil

1 Heat oven to 350°F. In medium skillet, cook sausage over medium heat; drain. Set aside to cool.

2 In medium bowl, combine salad dressing mix, mayonnaise and milk; mix well. Cover and refrigerate half of mixture for another use. To remaining mixture, add cheddar cheese, Monterey Jack cheese, bell pepper and olives; mix well. Add sausage; mix well. *(Recipe can be prepared to this point up to 1 day ahead. Cover and refrigerate.)*

3 Brush both sides of wonton skins lightly with oil. Press skins into miniature muffin tins to form cups. Bake 10 minutes or until golden brown. *(Wonton cups can be prepared up to 1 day ahead. Cover and refrigerate.)*

4 Place wonton cups on baking sheet. Fill cups with sausage mixture; bake 5 to 10 minutes or until cheese is melted and mixture is hot.

About 3 dozen wonton cups

PARMESAN CHEESE AND HERB CROSTINI

Priscilla Migliore
Sherman Oaks, California

30 slices baguette, cut diagonally (¼ inch thick)

¼ cup butter, melted

½ cup freshly shredded Parmesan cheese (2 oz.)

2 to 3 tablespoons finely chopped fresh rosemary

3 to 4 tablespoons extra-virgin olive oil

1 Heat oven to 400°F. Place baguette slices on baking sheet. Brush both sides lightly with butter. Sprinkle top side with cheese and rosemary; drizzle with oil.

2 Bake 10 minutes or until lightly toasted. Cool on wire rack.

30 appetizers

SUMMER MELON SMOOTHIE

Brian Bernhardt
Birmingham, Michigan

2 cups cubed summer melon (such as watermelon, honeydew or cantaloupe)*

1 cup ice cubes (5 to 7 cubes), crushed**

2 to 3 tablespoons powdered sugar

In blender, combine melon, ice and powdered sugar; cover and blend until smooth.

TIPS *Use ripe, super-sweet summer melons or recipe will taste rather bland. If desired, alcohol can be added.

**Place ice cubes in heavy-duty plastic bag and pound with mallet or hammer until coarsely crushed.

2 servings

CRAB-STUFFED MUSHROOM CAPS

Sharon Medbery
Chula Vista, California

24 large mushrooms

1 tablespoon butter

1 small onion, finely chopped

3 ribs celery, finely chopped

2 teaspoons minced garlic

1/4 teaspoon freshly ground pepper

1/4 teaspoon seasoned salt

15 oz. crabmeat, diced

2/3 cup seasoned bread crumbs

2 tablespoons freshly grated Parmesan cheese

2 tablespoons water

1/2 cup grated mozzarella cheese (2 oz.)

1 Heat oven to 350°F. Separate mushroom stems from caps. Chop stems; reserve 1/3 cup. Set aside.

2 In small skillet, melt butter over medium heat. Add onion, celery and 1/3 cup mushroom stems; sauté 4 to 5 minutes or until onion is tender. Add garlic, pepper and salt. Remove from heat.

3 In medium bowl, combine crab and mushroom stem mixture; mix well. Stir in bread crumbs and Parmesan cheese. Add enough water so filling sticks together but is not too moist.

4 Line 2 (15x10x1-inch) baking pans with parchment paper. Place mushroom caps on pans. Place a generous amount of filling in each cap. Sprinkle caps with mozzarella cheese. Bake 15 to 20 minutes or until caps are golden brown and cheese is melted.

24 mushroom caps

HOT OPEN-FACED ZUCCHINI SANDWICHES

Sylvia Owcarz
Plainfield, Illinois

2 cups shredded zucchini

1/2 teaspoon salt

1/2 cup mayonnaise

1/2 cup plain yogurt

1/4 cup freshly grated Parmesan cheese (1 oz.)

1/4 cup chopped green bell pepper

4 green onions, thinly sliced

1 garlic clove, minced

1 teaspoon Worcestershire sauce

1/4 teaspoon hot pepper sauce

36 slices snack rye bread

1 Heat oven to 375°F. In medium bowl, toss zucchini and salt. Let stand 1 hour. Rinse and drain. Add mayonnaise, yogurt, cheese, bell pepper, onions, garlic, Worcestershire sauce and hot pepper sauce; mix until well combined.

2 Spread scant 1 tablespoon or heaping teaspoon zucchini mixture on each bread slice. Place bread slices on 15x10x1-inch pan. Bake 10 to 12 minutes or until lightly browned.

3 dozen open-faced sandwiches

CRAB CHEESECAKE

CRAB CHEESECAKE

Richard Rands
Woodland Hills, Caliornia

CRUST

1 cup finely grated Parmesan cheese (4 oz.)

1 cup bread crumbs

1/2 cup butter, melted

FILLING

1 tablespoon olive oil

1 cup finely chopped onion

1/2 cup finely chopped green bell pepper

1/2 cup finely chopped red bell pepper

1 teaspoon minced garlic

1 cup finely chopped mushrooms

Salt

Freshly ground white pepper

3 (8-oz.) pkg. cream cheese

4 eggs

1/2 cup heavy orcam

1 tablespoon hot pepper sauce

1 cup grated Gouda cheese (4 oz.)

4 (6-oz.) cans crabmeat, drained

COULIS

3/4 cup chopped green onions

1/2 cup chopped fresh parsley

1/2 cup chopped fresh cilantro

1 tablespoon chopped shallot

1 tablespoon chopped garlic

1/4 teaspoon salt

1/4 teaspoon freshly ground black pepper

1/4 cup egg substitute

1 tablespoon balsamic vinegar

1/4 cup water

1 1/2 cups olive oil

1 Heat oven to 350°F. In medium bowl, combine Parmesan cheese, bread crumbs and butter; mix well. Press into bottom of 9-inch springform pan.

2 Heat 1 tablespoon oil in large skillet over medium-high heat until hot. Add onion, green bell pepper, red bell pepper and garlic; sauté 2 to 3 minutes. Add mushrooms, salt and white pepper; sauté an additional 2 to 3 minutes or until vegetables are tender. Remove from heat; set aside.

3 In large bowl, beat cream cheese and eggs at low speed until well mixed. Add cream, hot pepper sauce, Gouda cheese and sautéed vegetables; mix well. Fold in crabmeat. Pour into springform pan. Bake 1 hour to 1 hour and 15 minutes, or until internal temperature reaches 160°F.

4 Meanwhile, in blender, combine onions, parsley, cilantro, shallot, garlic, salt, blackpepper, egg substitute, and balsamic vinegar; blend until smooth. Alternately blend in water and 1 1/2 cups olive oil.

5 Remove cheesecake from oven; cool 1 hour. Refrigerate. Remove from springform pan; cut into wedges. Serve chilled with coulis.

12 servings

GLAZED PECANS

Gwendolyn Daugherty
Tonawanda, New York

- 2 egg whites
- 1 cup sugar
- Dash salt
- 3 cups pecans
- ½ cup butter, melted

1 Heat oven to 300°F. Grease 15x10x1-inch baking sheet. In medium bowl, beat egg whites at medium speed until stiff peaks form. Beat in sugar and salt. Fold in pecans and butter. Spread mixture on baking sheet.

2 Bake 20 to 25 minutes, stirring frequently. Pour onto another baking sheet. With two forks, stir and separate pecans until cool.

4 cups

SUN-DRIED TOMATO DIP

Gerda Pezzullo
Providence, Rhode Island

- ¼ cup sun-dried tomatoes in oil, drained, chopped
- 1 (8-oz.) pkg. cream cheese, softened
- ½ cup sour cream
- ½ cup mayonnaise
- ½ teaspoon hot pepper sauce
- ½ teaspoon kosher (coarse) salt
- ⅛ teaspoon freshly ground pepper
- 2 green onions, thinly sliced

In food processor, combine tomatoes, cream cheese, sour cream, mayonnaise, hot pepper sauce, salt and pepper; pulse until smooth. Add green onions; pulse twice.

2¼ cups

GINGER CRAB CAKES

Charlene Rands
Woodland Hills, California

- ½ teaspoon light olive oil
- 1 garlic clove, minced
- 1 medium jalapeño chile, finely chopped
- 2 tablespoons finely chopped red onion
- 2 tablespoons finely chopped red bell pepper
- 2 tablespoons finely chopped celery
- 2 tablespoons minced fresh ginger
- 1 (6-oz.) can crabmeat
- ½ cup unseasoned bread crumbs
- 1 egg, beaten
- 2 tablespoons soy sauce
- 2 teaspoons sesame oil
- 1 teaspoon hot pepper sauce
- Salt
- Freshly ground pepper

COATING
- ½ cup all-purpose flour
- 1 egg, beaten
- 1 cup panko bread crumbs*
- ¼ cup vegetable oil
- 1 tablespoon finely chopped parsley

1 Heat oil in small skillet over medium-high heat until hot. Add garlic, chile, onion, bell pepper, celery and 1 tablespoon of the ginger; sauté 2 minutes. Remove from heat; cool.

2 In large bowl, combine cooled pepper mixture, remaining 1 tablespoon ginger, crabmeat, unseasoned bread crumbs, 1 beaten egg, soy sauce, sesame oil, hot pepper sauce, salt and pepper; mix well. Divide mixture into 4 portions; shape each portion into 3-inch-round cake. Place on baking sheet; refrigerate 30 minutes.

3 Dredge each patty in flour; dip in beaten egg. Dip in panko bread crumbs.

4 Heat large skillet over medium-high heat until hot. Add vegetable oil; heat until hot. Fry patties 4 minutes or until golden brown, turning once. Garnish with parsley.

TIP *Look for panko bread crumbs in the ethnic section of the grocery store or in an Asian market.

4 crab cakes

BLACK BEAN SALSA

Rosemary Siewert
Apple Valley, Minnesota

1 (15-oz.) can black beans, drained, rinsed

1 cup corn

1 cup tomatoes, seeded, diced

1/2 cup chopped green onions

2 tablespoons fresh lime juice

1 tablespoon olive oil

2 tablespoons diced fresh cilantro

1 teaspoon ground cumin

1/2 teaspoon salt

1/2 teaspoon freshly ground pepper

1/2 jalapeño pepper, seeded, minced

In large bowl, combine beans, corn, tomatoes, onions, lime juice, olive oil, cilantro, cumin, salt, pepper and jalapeño; mix well. Serve with tortilla chips.

8 (1/2-cup) servings

KEY LIME CITRUS FREEZE

Connie Husband
Belle Fourche, South Dakota

2 (6-oz.) containers Key lime yogurt

1 (12-oz.) can frozen lemonade, thawed

3 tablespoons light corn syrup

2 teaspoons grated lemon or orange peel

2 cups lemon-lime carbonated beverage

1 In large bowl, whisk together yogurt, lemonade, corn syrup and lemon. Cover and freeze 6 to 8 hours or until of slushy consistency, stirring occasionally.

2 Stir in carbonated beverage; serve over ice.

4 servings

TANGERINE TANGO

Lara Moody
Columbia, Missouri

2 cups tangerine juice

1 cup orange sherbet

1/2 to 1 cup vodka, to taste

2 cups ice cubes (about 10 to 14 cubes)

In blender, combine juice, sherbet, vodka and ice; blend well, allowing ice cubes to be crushed completely.

5 (1-cup) servings

POTATO BALLS

Lori Kennison
Jacksonville, Florida

4 large potatoes, cooked, mashed

10 slices bacon, fried crisp, drained, crumbled

1/2 cup butter, melted

2 large green onions, finely chopped

1 teaspoon salt

1 cup all-purpose flour

2 eggs, beaten

Sliced almonds

4 cups vegetable oil

1 In large bowl, combine potatoes, bacon, butter, onions and salt; mix well. Refrigerate at least 2 hours.

2 Shape potato mixture into 1-inch balls. Roll in flour; dip in eggs. Roll in sliced almonds.

3 In large saucepan, heat oil to 375°F. Deep-fry potato balls until golden; drain on paper towels. Serve hot.

64 potato balls

MINI QUICHE CUPS

Kyra Taylor
Dexter, Missouri

| 1 lb. mild sausage, cooked, drained
| 2 cups half-and-half
| 1 lb. pasteurized process cheese spread, cubed
| 7 eggs, beaten
| ¼ teaspoon salt
| ¼ teaspoon ground red pepper
| ¼ teaspoon ground cumin

1 Heat oven to 350°F. Spray mini muffin pans with nonstick cooking spray. In large saucepan, combine sausage, half-and-half and cheese; cook over medium heat 10 minutes or until cheese is melted, stirring occaionally. Remove from heat.

2 Add eggs, salt, pepper and cumin; mix well. Spoon into muffin cups. Bake 20 to 25 minutes or until firm and golden brown on top.

5 dozen mini quiches

MY FAVORITE BRUSCHETTA

Robin Konstanz
West Bend, Wisconsin

| 1½ large tomatoes, seeded, diced
| ½ small onion, diced
| 2 tablespoons chopped fresh basil
| 2 tablespoons capers
| 2 garlic cloves, minced
| 2 tablespoons olive oil
| 1 loaf French bread, cut into ½-inch slices
| ½ cup freshly grated Parmesan cheese (2 oz.)

1 In medium bowl, combine tomatoes, onion, basil, capers and garlic; mix well. Add oil; mix gently. Cover and refrigerate 1 to 2 hours.

2 Heat broiler. Place bread slices on broiler pan. Broil 1 to 2 minutes or until light brown; turn over. Spread each slice with 2 teaspoons tomato mixture; top with ½ to 1 teaspoon cheese. Broil an additional 1 to 2 minutes or until cheese is melted.

38 appetizers

SUMMERTIME SUN PUNCH

Jeff and Abby Wilson
Minneapolis, Minnesota

| 1 cup fresh orange juice
| 1 cup lemonade
| 4 cups cold water
| 1 quart chilled white carbonated beverage
| 1 orange, thinly sliced

In 3-quart container, combine orange juice, lemonade, water and carbonated beverage; mix well. Serve in punch bowl with ice; top with orange slices.

2½ quarts

HUMMUS

Joan Deady
San Francisco, California

| 1 (15-oz.) can garbanzo beans, drained
| 2 teaspoons olive oil
| 2 tablespoons fresh lemon juice
| 1 teaspoon chili oil
| 4 cloves garlic, minced

1 Process beans, oil, lemon juice, chili oil and garlic in food processor. Blend until smooth.

2 Serve with pita pockets, fresh-cut vegetables or bread sticks.

2½ cups

MY FAVORITE BRUSCHETTA

ZUCCHINI SQUARES

Laurianne Rembisz
Midlothian, Virginia

- 4 medium zucchini, grated (about 4 cups)
- 1 teaspoon salt
- 1/2 medium onion, finely chopped
- 1 cup grated cheddar cheese (4 oz.)
- 3/4 cups buttermilk baking mix
- 1/2 cup vegetable oil
- 2 eggs, beaten
- 1 tablespoon minced fresh basil

1 Heat oven to 350°F. Place zucchini in medium bowl; sprinkle with salt. Let stand 45 minutes. Squeeze and drain.

2 In large bowl, combine zucchini, onion, cheese, baking mix, oil, eggs and basil; mix well. Pour into 9x7-inch pan. Bake 30 minutes. Cool 10 minutes; cut into 1-inch squares.

48 servings

MELISSA'S SALSA

Melissa Mehaffey
Delta Junction, Alaska

- 2 tablespoons tomato paste
- 1/4 cup water
- 4 cups chopped tomatoes
- 1/2 cup chopped bell pepper
- 1/4 cup chopped jalapeño or serrano chiles
- 1 small onion, diced
- 2 garlic cloves, diced
- 2 teaspoons fresh lime juice
- 2 teaspoons red wine vinegar
- 2 teaspoons chili powder
- 3/4 teaspoon salt
- 1/8 teaspoon sugar
- 1/8 teaspoon cumin
- Pinch oregano

In medium bowl, combine tomato paste and water; mix well. Stir in tomatoes. Add bell pepper, chiles, onion, garlic, lime juice, vinegar, chili powder, salt, sugar, cumin and oregano; mix well. Serve immediately or store in refrigerator.

5 1/4 cups

FANCY HOT ARTICHOKE DIP

Tansy Lovato
Spokane, Washington

- 2 cups mayonnaise
- 2 cups shredded Pepper Jack cheese (8 oz.)
- 2 cups shredded Parmesan cheese (8 oz.)
- 2 (6.5-oz.) jars marinated artichoke hearts, drained
- 2 baguettes, cut into 1-inch slices

1 Heat oven to 350°F. Grease 9-inch gratin dish. Add mayonnaise, Pepper Jack cheese and Parmesan cheese; mix well.

2 With grapefruit spoon or fingers, scoop out artichoke hearts; drain slightly and place on top of cheeses. Bake uncovered, 25 minutes or until hot and bubbly. Serve with baguette slices.

8 to 10 servings

CUCUMBER DIP

Jeff and Abby Wilson
Minneapolis, Minnesota

2 (8-oz.) pkg. cream cheese, softened

½ cup green onions, chopped

1 large cucumber, seeded, grated

1 tablespoon fresh lemon juice

1 teaspoon minced garlic

In large mixing bowl, combine cream cheese, onions, cucumber, lemon juice and garlic; beat at medium speed until smooth. Refrigerate 1 hour. Serve with chips.

2 cups

ROASTED RED PEPPER & GARLIC SPREAD

Dick and Ginger Howell
Pittsford, New York

6 medium red bell peppers

2 garlic cloves

¼ cup olive oil

½ cup freshly grated Parmesan cheese (2 oz.)

Salt

Freshly ground pepper

2 large loaves ciabatta bread

1 Heat oven to 400°F. Place peppers on baking sheet; bake 20 to 25 minutes or until charred. Place in resealable plastic bag; seal bag. Let stand 15 minutes or until cool enough to handle. Peel peppers under running water, removing charred skin. Remove veins and seeds. Reduce oven temperature to 375°F.

2 Place peppers in food processor; process until finely chopped. Add garlic, oil, cheese, salt and pepper; puree until well combined.

3 Place bread on baking sheet. Bake 10 to 15 minutes to warm. Slice and serve with pepper spread.

3 cups

PARTY HAM ROLLS

Rosemary Siewert
Apple Valley, Minnesota

1 cup butter, melted

3 tablespoons brown mustard

1½ to 2 tablespoons poppy seeds

1 medium onion, diced

1 teaspoon Worcestershire sauce

12 to 16 party-style or brown-and-serve-style rolls

½ lb. country-style ham, sliced

6 to 8 slices Swiss cheese

1 Heat oven to 300°F. In small bowl, combine butter, mustard, poppy seeds, onion and Worcestershire sauce. Slice rolls almost all the way through. Spread each half of roll with mustard mixture. Place layer of ham on bottom half of roll. Top with layer of cheese and another layer of ham. Close rolls.

2 Return rolls to tray in which they came or place on shallow baking sheet. Cover with foil. Bake 20 minutes or until heated through. To serve, cut rolls in half.

12 to 16 servings

PESTO TOASTS

Fred Schmidtke
Wake Forest, North Carolina

¾ cup chopped fresh basil

1 garlic clove

¼ cup olive oil

½ cup freshly grated Parmesan cheese (2 oz.)

3 tablespoons mayonnaise

Salt

Freshly ground pepper

1 baguette, cut into 24 (⅓-inch) slices

1 Heat oven to 400°F. To make pesto in food processor, combine basil and garlic; process until finely chopped. With machine running, add oil through feed tube; process until smooth. Add cheese; pulse until combined. Place mixture in small bowl. Whisk in mayonnaise; season with salt and pepper.

2 Place bread slices on baking sheet. Bake 4 to 6 minutes or until golden brown; turn over. Spread pesto on untoasted sides, leaving ¼-inch border around edges. Broil until pesto bubbles.

24 appetizers

TOMATILLO SALSA

Tansy Lovato
Spokane, Washington

10 tomatillos

1 small tomato, chopped

½ small red onion, chopped

6 cloves garlic, minced

4 jalepeño chiles, seeded, finely chopped

1 cup coarsely chopped fresh pineapple

¼ cup chopped fresh cilantro

¾ teaspoon salt

2 teaspoons fresh lime juice

1 Remove and discard husks from tomatillo. In large bowl, combine tomatillos, tomato, onion, garlic, chiles, pineapple, cilantro, salt and lime juice.

2 Cover and refrigerate salsa 1 hour before serving.

2½ cups

Breads

KIMBERLY'S LOW-FAT CRANBERRY-APPLE BREAD

Kimberly Antal
Longmeadow, Massachusetts

½ cup packed brown sugar

¼ cup sugar

2 tablespoons canola oil

1 egg

2 cups peeled chopped apples

1½ cups whole wheat flour

1½ teaspoons baking powder

1 teaspoon cinnamon

⅛ to ¼ teaspoon ground cloves

1 cup cranberries

½ cup chopped walnuts or slivered almonds

1 Heat oven to 350°F. Spray 8x4-inch loaf pan with nonstick cooking spray.

2 In medium bowl, combine brown sugar, sugar and oil; beat at medium speed until well blended. Add egg; beat again. Stir in apples.

3 In another medium bowl, combine flour, baking powder, cinnamon and cloves; mix well. Add flour mixture to apple mixture; mix well. Fold in cranberries and walnuts. Spread batter evenly into pan.

4 Bake 1 hour or until toothpick inserted near center comes out clean. Cool 10 minutes. Remove from pan; cool completely on wire rack.

1 (12-slice) loaf

CREAM BISCUITS

Lori Kennison
Jacksonville, Florida

2 cups self-rising flour

1 cup heavy cream*

2 tablespoons butter, melted

1 Heat oven to 450°F. Line baking sheet with parchment paper. In medium bowl, beat flour and cream until stiff dough forms, adding 1 to 2 tablespoons water if needed.

2 On lightly floured surface, knead dough 10 to 12 times. Roll out dough to ½ inch thickness. With 2½-inch biscuit cutter, cut out 10 rounds. Place rounds on baking sheet; lightly brush with melted butter. Bake 10 to 12 minutes or until light golden brown.

TIP *1 (8-oz.) container sour cream may be used in place of the heavy cream.

10 biscuits

CHEESE BREAD

Noble King
Stockton, Missouri

1 (¼- oz.) pkg. active dry yeast

1 cup warm reduced-sodium chicken or vegetable broth (110°F to 115°F)

1 tablespoon margarine

3 cups all-purpose flour

2 tablespoons sugar

½ teaspoon salt

1 egg, beaten

1 cup finely shredded cheddar cheese (4 oz.)

1 In medium bowl, dissolve yeast in broth. Add margarine, 1 cup of the flour, sugar, salt and egg; beat until smooth. Add cheese and remaining 2 cups flour; stir until well mixed. Cover; let rise in warm place 30 minutes or until double in size.

2 Heat oven to 375°F. Grease 9x5x3-inch loaf pan. Knead dough in bowl by hand 25 strokes. Place in pan. Cover; let rise 30 minutes or until double in size.

3 Bake 30 minutes or until golden brown. Cool 10 minutes. Remove from pan; cool completely on wire rack.

1 (16-slice) loaf

MARLENE'S SOFT WHITE SANDWICH BREAD FOR BREAD MACHINES

Marlene Sinyard
Brunswick, Maine

1 cup water

3 tablespoons honey

3 cups all-purpose flour

1/4 cup instant potato granules

1/4 cup powdered buttermilk

1 1/2 teaspoons salt

2 tablespoons butter

2 teaspoons yeast

1 Follow manufacturer's instructions for placing ingredients into bread pan. Select basic light or sandwich setting; start machine.

2 When bread is done baking, turn out onto wire rack. Cover with towel until cooled.

1 (1 1/2-lb.) loaf

LEMON-POPPY SEED BREAD

Rosemary Siewert
Apple Valley, Minnesota

1 pkg. lemon or yellow cake mix

2 (4-oz.) pkg. instant coconut cream pudding

4 eggs

1 cup hot water (115°F to 120°F)

1/2 cup canola oil

1 (1.25-oz.) container poppy seeds (1/4 cup)

Heat oven to 350°F. Grease and flour 2 (8x4-inch) loaf pans. In large bowl, combine cake mix, pudding, eggs, water, oil and poppy seeds; mix well. Bake 40 to 50 minutes or until toothpick inserted near center comes out clean.

2 (8-slice) loaves

COUSIN ADA'S BUTTERFLAKE ROLLS

Joanna Henry
Houston, Texas

1 pkg. active dry yeast

1/2 cup warm water (110°F to 115°F)

2 eggs

1/2 cup sugar

1 1/4 cups canned evaporated milk

1 cup hot water (115°F to 120°F)

2 teaspoons salt

6 to 8 cups all-purpose flour

6 tablespoons butter, softened

1 In small bowl, combine yeast and warm water. Let stand 5 minutes or until yeast foams. In large bowl, beat eggs and sugar at medium speed 30 seconds or until well mixed. Add yeast mixture, milk and hot water; blend briefly to mix. Add salt; mix well. Beat in 3 cups flour; add remaining flour 1 cup at a time until dough is very stiff but still smooth. Knead on lightly floured surface 8 to 12 minutes or until smooth and elastic, adding flour as needed.

2 Spray 4 muffin tins and 1 (9-inch) pie plate with nonstick cooking spray. Roll out dough to 1/2 inch thickness; spread with 1 1/2 tablespoons of the butter. Fold dough over and roll to 1/2 inch thickness; spread with 1 1/2 tablespoons of the butter. Repeat folding, rolling and buttering two more times. Fold dough over one last time; roll to 1/2 inch thickness.

3 With cookie cutter or glass the same diameter as the bottom of the muffin tins, cut dough into circles. Place circles in muffin tins, 1 circle per cup. Press unused dough into pie plate. Cover; let rise 3 to 4 hours.

4 Heat oven to 425°F. Place muffin tins on center oven rack; bake 5 to 8 minutes or until light brown and cooked all the way through. Cool on wire racks. Reduce oven temperature to 400°F. Cook dough in pie plate 17 to 20 minutes or until lightly browned and cooked all the way through. Cool on wire rack.

4 dozen rolls and 1 (8-inch) round loaf

GREEN CHILE CORN BREAD

GREEN CHILE CORN BREAD

Roseann Ilstrup
Lakeside, California

¾ cup butter

1 cup yellow cornmeal

1 tablespoon sugar

4 eggs

1½ cups all-purpose flour

1 tablespoon baking powder

1½ teaspoons salt

1 (15-oz.) can creamed corn

1 (4-oz.) can chopped green chiles

⅓ cup grated cheddar cheese

⅓ cup grated Monterey Jack cheese

1 Heat oven to 375°F. Spray 8-inch square pan with nonstick cooking spray. In large bowl, beat butter, cornmeal and sugar at medium speed until well blended. Add eggs one at a time, beating well after each addition.

2 In small bowl, combine flour, baking powder and salt. Add to cornmeal mixture; mix well. Stir in corn, chiles, cheddar cheese and Monterey Jack cheese. Pour batter into pan. Bake 45 minutes or until toothpick inserted near center comes out clean. Cool slightly. Cut into squares.

9 servings

CHOCOLATE CHUNK BANANA BREAD

Laura Adderley
Birmingham, Michigan

1¾ cups packed brown sugar

1½ cups butter or margarine, softened

4 eggs

1½ teaspoons grated orange peel

2½ teaspoons vanilla

½ teaspoon almond extract

4 cups all-purpose flour

1 tablespoon baking powder

1 teaspoon salt

2 teaspoons cinnamon

1 teaspoon nutmeg

½ teaspoon baking soda

2 cups mashed ripe bananas

1 cup cold strong black coffee

1 (12-oz.) pkg. chocolate chunks

1 Heat oven to 350°F. Generously spray 2 (8x4- or 9x5-inch) loaf pans with nonstick cooking spray.

2 In large bowl, combine brown sugar and butter; beat until well blended. Add eggs one at a time, beating well after each addition; beat until fluffy. Stir in orange peel, vanilla and almond extract.

3 In medium bowl, combine flour, baking powder, salt, cinnamon, nutmeg and baking soda; mix well. In another medium bowl, stir together bananas and coffee. Add dry ingredients to butter mixture alternately with banana mixture, beginning and ending with dry ingredients. Mix just until dry ingredients are moistened; do not overmix. Stir in chocolate chunks. Spread batter evenly in pans.

4 Bake 8x4-inch pans 1¼ to 1½ hours; bake 9x5-inch pans 50 to 60 minutes or until toothpick inserted near center comes out clean. Cool 10 minutes. Remove from pans; place on wire racks. Cool at least 1 hour before slicing.

2 (16-slice) loaves

CARAMEL ROLLS WITH SWEET DOUGH

Rosemary Siewert
Apple Valley, Minnesota

DOUGH

1 (¹/4-oz.) pkg. active dry yeast

¹/2 cup plus 2 tablespoons warm water (105°F to 115°F)

¹/2 teaspoon sugar

¹/2 cup milk

¹/2 cup mashed potatoes, strained to remove lumps, reserving ¹/2 cup cooking water

6 tablespoons margarine

¹/4 cup plus 2 tablespoons sugar

1 teaspoon salt

1 egg

1 egg yolk

4 to 4¹/2 cups all-purpose flour

TOPPING

1 cup packed brown sugar

2 teaspoons cinnamon

¹/4 cup plus 2 tablespoons butter

8 teaspoons half-and-half

¹/2 cup chopped pecans

1 In small bowl, combine yeast, water and sugar. Let stand about 10 minutes or until yeast foams.

2 In medium saucepan, heat milk and ¹/2 cup reserved cooking water until mixture is scalded; remove from heat. Stir in mashed potatoes, margarine, sugar and salt; cool until mixture is lukewarm.

3 In large bowl, mix egg and egg yolk until well beaten. Add milk mixture, yeast mixture and 1 cup of the flour; beat at medium speed 5 minutes. Mix in remaining flour 1 cup at a time until soft dough forms. Place in greased bowl; cover. Let rise until 2¹/2 times original size, about 2 hours.

4 Spray 13x9-inch pan with nonstick cooking spray. In small bowl, combine ¹/3 cup brown sugar and cinnamon. On floured surface, roll dough into rectangle 10 inches across and from ¹/2 to ¹/4 inch thick. Melt 2 tablespoons butter; brush on dough. Sprinkle brown sugar mixture over dough.

5 Roll up dough starting from long end. Pinch dough together at seam, using small amount of water to seal. Cut dough into 1-inch pieces.

6 In medium saucepan, combine ²/3 cup brown sugar, ¹/4 cup butter and half-and-half; heat until bubbly. Pour into pan. Sprinkle with pecans. Place dough on top of pecans; cover with towel. Let rise 30 minutes or until doubled in size.

7 Heat oven to 350°F. Bake dough 25 to 30 minutes or until brown on top. Invert onto wire rack or serving plate.

16 large rolls

CHOCOLATE ZUCCHINI BREAD

Jeannette Walker
Flint, Michigan

3 cups all-purpose flour

1/4 cup unsweetened cocoa

1 tablespoon cinnamon

1 teaspoon baking soda

1/2 teaspoon baking powder

1 teaspoon salt

2 cups sugar

3 eggs

1 cup vegetable oil

2 teaspoons vanilla

2 cups grated zucchini

1 cup chopped nuts

1 cup semisweet chocolate chunks

1 Heat oven to 350°F. Grease 2 (8x4-inch) loaf pans. In large bowl, combine flour, cocoa, cinnamon, baking soda, baking powder and salt; mix well. Set aside.

2 In medium bowl, combine sugar and eggs; beat until well blended. Add oil and vanilla; beat until combined. Stir in zucchini. Add flour mixture; stir just until moistened. Stir in nuts and chocolate chunks. Divide and spoon batter evenly into loaf pans.

3 Bake 55 to 60 minutes or until toothpick inserted near center comes out clean. Cool in pans 10 minutes. Remove breads from pans; cool completely on wire racks.

2 (18-slice) loaves

CHOCOLATE CHIP-PECAN BREAD FOR BREAD MACHINES

Marlene Sinyard
Brunswick, Maine

1 1/2 cups water

1 egg

1/2 cup whole wheat flour

3 cups bread flour

1/3 cup sugar

1 1/2 teaspoons salt

2 tablespoons butter

2 teaspoons yeast

1 cup chocolate chips

3/4 cup pecans

1 Follow manufacturer's instructions for placing all ingredients except pecans and chocolate chips into bread pan. Select sweet,* medium crust settings; start machine. Add pecans and chocolate chips when machine beeps, indicating ingredients can be added.

2 When bread is done baking, turn out onto wire rack. Cool completely before slicing.

TIP *Choose the setting on your bread machine that allows ingredients to be added during kneading cycle.

1 (1 1/2-lb.) loaf

BANANA BREAD

Shar Stanton
Bowling Green, Ohio

½ cup butter

1 cup sugar

2 eggs

1 teaspoon grated lemon peel

2 cups all-purpose flour

½ teaspoon baking powder

½ teaspoon salt

½ teaspoon baking soda

1 teaspoon cinnamon

3 bananas, mashed (about 1½ cups)

1 cup pecans

1 Heat oven to 350°F. Spray 9x5-inch loaf pan with nonstick cooking spray.

2 In large bowl, combine butter and sugar; beat until well blended. Add eggs one at a time, beating well after each addition; beat until fluffy. Stir in lemon peel.

3 In medium bowl, combine flour, baking powder, salt, baking soda and cinnamon; mix well. Add dry ingredients to butter mixture alternately with bananas, beginning and ending with dry ingredients. Mix just until dry ingredients are moistened; do not overmix. Stir in pecans. Pour into pan.

4 Bake 65 minutes or until toothpick inserted near center comes out clean. Cool 10 minutes. Remove from pan; cool on wire rack at least 1 hour before slicing.

1 (16-slice) loaf

PUMPKIN-BANANA MUFFINS

Kimberly Antal
Longmeadow, Massachusetts

1½ cups sugar

½ cup vegetable oil

2 eggs, beaten

¾ cup canned pumpkin

¼ cup mashed banana

⅓ cup water

2 cups all-purpose flour

1 teaspoon salt

¾ teaspoon baking soda

½ teaspoon baking powder

½ teaspoon cinnamon

½ teaspoon ground cloves

½ teaspoon nutmeg

¼ teaspoon ginger

½ cup golden raisins

1 Heat oven to 350°F. Spray 12 muffin cups with nonstick cooking spray. In medium bowl, combine sugar and oil; mix well. Add eggs; mix until combined. Add pumpkin, banana and water; mix well.

2 In large bowl, combine flour, salt, baking soda, baking powder, cinnamon, cloves, nutmeg and ginger. Add pumpkin mixture, stirring just until moistened. Fold in raisins. Pour batter into muffin cups. Bake 30 minutes or until toothpick inserted near center comes out clean. Cool on wire racks.

16 muffins

PUMPKIN-BANANA MUFFINS

HOT CINNAMON ROLLS

Barbara Johnson
Marina, California

DOUGH

¾ cup milk

½ cup sugar

¾ cup butter

2 (¼-oz.) pkg. active dry yeast

½ cup warm water (110°F to 115°F)

⅛ teaspoon salt

5¾ cups all-purpose flour

1 (3.4-oz.) pkg. French vanilla instant pudding

2 eggs, beaten

1 tablespoon vanilla

1 cup sour cream

FILLING

½ cup sugar

½ cup packed brown sugar

1½ tablespoons cinnamon

⅛ teaspoon nutmeg

¾ cup raisins

¾ cup pecans

TOPPING

1 (3-oz.) pkg. cream cheese

1½ cups sifted powdered sugar

2 tablespoons milk

1 teaspoon vanilla

1 In small saucepan, combine ¾ cup milk, ½ cup sugar and ½ cup of the butter; mix well. Heat over low heat until butter melts. Cool.

2 In large bowl, dissolve yeast in water; add salt. Let stand 5 minutes. Stir in milk mixture; let stand an additional 5 minutes.

3 In another large bowl, combine 4½ cups flour and pudding; mix well. In medium bowl, combine eggs, 1 tablespoon vanilla and sour cream; mix well. Alternately add flour mixture and egg mixture to yeast mixture, beating at medium speed.

4 Turn dough out onto lightly floured surface; knead until smooth, adding additional flour when necessary. Place in well-greased bowl, turning to grease top of dough. Cover; let rise in warm place free from drafts 1 hour or until double in size.

5 Melt remaining ¼ cup butter. Punch dough; divide in half. On lightly floured surface, roll each half into a 16x10-inch rectangle. Brush each half with butter.

6 Grease 2 (13x9-inch) pans. In medium bowl, combine sugar, brown sugar, cinnamon, nutmeg, raisins and pecans; mix well. Sprinkle half of mixture over each rectangle. Roll up dough starting from long end. Pinch dough together at the seam, using small amount of water to seal. Cut dough into 1-inch slices; arrange in pans ¼ inch apart. Cover; let rise in warm place free from drafts 1 hour or until double in size.

7 Heat oven to 350°F. Bake rolls 20 to 30 minutes or until light brown.

8 To make topping, in another medium bowl, combine cream cheese, powdered sugar, milk and vanilla; mix until smooth. Spread over warm rolls.

32 rolls

TROPICAL LIME BREAD

Cheryl Flandrena
Marlborough, Massachusetts

BREAD

$1/2$ cup unsalted butter, softened

1 cup sugar

2 eggs

1 teaspoon grated lime peel

3 tablespoons fresh lime juice

$1/4$ cup finely chopped dried pineapple

$1/4$ cup finely chopped dried papaya

$1^3/4$ cups all-purpose flour

$1^1/4$ teaspoons baking powder

$1/2$ teaspoon salt

1 teaspoon ground ginger

$1/2$ teaspoon ground cardamom

$1/4$ teaspoon ground allspice

$1/2$ cup milk

GLAZE

$1/3$ cup sugar

3 tablespoons fresh lime juice

1 teaspoon grated lime peel

1 Heat oven to 350°F. Grease 8x4-inch loaf pan. In large bowl, combine butter and 1 cup sugar; beat at medium-high speed until light and fluffy. Add eggs one at a time, beating well after each addition. Add 1 teaspoon lime peel and 3 tablespoons lime juice; mix well.

2 In small bowl, combine pineapple and papaya. Add 1 tablespoon of the flour; toss to combine. Set aside.

3 In medium bowl, combine remaining flour, baking powder, salt, ginger, cardamom and allspice; mix well. Add flour mixture and milk alternately to butter mixture, mixing until combined. Stir in pineapple mixture. Spoon into pan.

4 Bake 55 to 60 minutes or until toothpick inserted near center comes out clean. Cool on wire rack 10 minutes.

5 Meanwhile, make glaze. In small saucepan, combine $1/3$ cup sugar and 3 tablespoons lime juice. Bring to a boil over medium heat; boil until sugar is dissolved. Stir in 1 teaspoon grated lime peel. Spoon hot glaze over bread. Cool bread in pan on wire rack an additional 30 minutes. Remove bread from pan. Place on wire rack; cool completely.

1 (16-slice) loaf

RHUBARB BREAD

Shar Stanton
Bowling Green, Ohio

2 cups diced fresh rhubarb

$1^1/2$ cups sugar

1 cup vegetable oil

$1/2$ cup milk

3 eggs

3 cups plus 2 tablespoons all-purpose flour

2 teaspoons baking soda

$1/2$ teaspoon baking powder

$1/2$ teaspoon salt

1 tablespoon cinnamon

1 Heat oven to 325°F. Grease 2 (9x4x2-inch) loaf pans. In blender, combine rhubarb, sugar, oil, milk and eggs; process until smooth.

2 In large bowl, combine flour, baking soda, baking powder, salt and cinnamon; mix well. Slowly add rhubarb mixture to flour mixture; stir just until dry ingredients are moistened.

3 Pour half of batter into each loaf pan. Bake 1 hour or until toothpick inserted near center comes out clean. Cool 10 minutes. Remove from pans; place on wire racks.

2 (16-slice) loaves

CRANBERRY ZUCCHINI BREAD

CRANBERRY ZUCCHINI BREAD

Bonnie Bowers
Volcano, California

5 eggs, beaten

2$\frac{1}{2}$ cups sugar

1$\frac{1}{4}$ cup vegetable oil

4 cups firmly packed shredded zucchini

1 tablespoon plus 1 teaspoon vanilla

3 cups all-purpose flour

1 tablespoon cinnamon

1 teaspoon ground cloves

1$\frac{1}{2}$ teaspoons salt

1$\frac{1}{2}$ teaspoons baking soda

$\frac{1}{2}$ teaspoon baking powder

1 cup chopped walnuts or pecans

1 cup dried cranberries

1 Heat oven to 325°F. Spray 2 (9x5x3-inch) loaf pans with nonstick cooking spray. Line bottom of pans with parchment paper; spray with nonstick cooking spray.

2 In large bowl, combine eggs, sugar and oil; beat until well blended. Add zucchini and vanilla; mix well. Add flour, cinnamon, cloves, salt, baking soda and baking powder; beat at medium speed until well blended. Stir in walnuts and cranberries; pour into pans.

3 Bake 50 to 70 minutes or until toothpick inserted near center comes out clean. Cool in pans 10 minutes; turn out onto wire racks. Peel off parchment paper.

2 (16-slice) loaves

DRIED FRUIT BREAD FOR BREAD MACHINES

Marlene Sinyard
Brunswick, Maine

$\frac{2}{3}$ cup mixed dried fruit

2 tablespoons rum

1 cup water

3 cups all-purpose flour

2 tablespoons powdered milk

3 tablespoons sugar

1$\frac{1}{2}$ teaspoons salt

1$\frac{1}{2}$ teaspoons cinnamon

2 tablespoons butter

2 teaspoons yeast

1 In small bowl, plump dried fruit by soaking in rum.

2 Follow manufacturer's instructions for placing all ingredients except dried fruit and rum into bread pan; select sweet,* light crust settings. Start machine. Add fruit and rum when machine beeps, indicating ingredients can be added.

3 When bread is done baking, turn out onto wire rack. Cool.

TIP *Choose the setting on your bread machine that allows ingredients to be added during kneading cycle.

1 (1$\frac{1}{2}$-lb.) loaf

JALAPEÑO CHEESE BISCUITS

Cecelia Rooney
Point Pleasant, New Jersey

2 cups all-purpose flour

4 teaspoons baking powder

1/2 teaspoon salt

1/4 teaspoon sugar

1/2 cup unsalted butter, chilled, cut up

3/4 cup half-and-half

1 cup grated Monterey Jack cheese with jalapeño chiles (4 oz.)

1 Heat oven to 425°F. Line baking sheet with parchment paper. In large bowl, sift together flour, baking powder, salt and sugar. With pastry blender or two knives, cut butter into flour mixture until mixture crumbles.

2 Add half-and-half to butter mixture; mix well. Stir in cheese. On lightly floured surface, knead dough 30 seconds. Pat into 1-inch-thick disk. Cut into rounds with 2-inch round biscuit or cookie cutter. Place on baking sheet.

3 Bake 15 minutes or until rounds are puffed and golden. Cool on wire rack.

12 biscuits

BLUEBERRY MUFFINS

Greg Bauer
Clinton, Missouri

1 1/2 cups all-purpose flour

3/4 cup sugar

1 1/2 teaspoons baking powder

1/4 teaspoon salt

1/2 teaspoon cinnamon

1 large egg

1/2 cup milk

6 tablespoons butter, melted

1 1/2 cups blueberries

Sugar

1 Heat oven to 400°F. Spray 12 muffin cups with nonstick cooking spray. In large bowl, combine flour, sugar, baking powder, salt and cinnamon; mix well.

2 In medium bowl, beat egg, milk and butter at medium speed until frothy. Add to flour mixture; stir just until combined. Fold in blueberries. Pour batter into muffin cups.

3 Bake 25 minutes or until tops are browned. During last 10 minutes of baking, sprinkle muffins with sugar. Remove from pan; cool slightly on wire rack.

12 muffins

Soups & Salads

ITALIAN WEDDING SOUP

Spirit Goodavage
Chloe, West Virginia

1 lb. fresh spinach, cut into ½-inch strips*
⅛ teaspoon plus pinch salt
2 tablespoons olive oil
½ onion, diced
1 garlic clove, diced
1½ quarts chicken stock
2 chicken bouillon cubes
½ cup acine di pepe (small Italian pasta) or orzo
Grated cheese

1 Place spinach and ⅛ teaspoon salt in large Dutch oven or large pot; cover. Cook over medium heat, adding no water except that which is clinging to the spinach leaves. When water from spinach begins to bubble, cook an additional 2 minutes.

2 Heat oil in medium saucepan over medium-high heat until hot. Add onion and garlic; sauté 3 to 4 minutes. Add spinach, spinach liquid and ½ cup of the stock. Cover; bring to a boil. Reduce heat to medium; simmer, covered, about 30 minutes or until spinach is tender.

3 Meanwhile, in same Dutch oven or large pot, bring remaining stock and bouillon cubes to a boil; add pasta. Return to a boil; cook an additional 10 minutes or until pasta is al dente. Combine pasta and spinach mixture. Sprinkle with cheese.

TIP *Frozen spinach can be substituted. Add with stock to sautéed onion and garlic; simmer, covered, 10 minutes.

8 (1-cup) servings

WARM CANNELLINI BEAN SALAD

Judy Kosloski
St. Clair Shores, Michigan

1 (19-oz.) can cannellini beans, drained, rinsed
1 rib celery with leaf top, finely chopped
1 tablespoon chopped red onion
3 tablespoons olive oil
2 tablespoons red wine vinegar
1 small garlic clove, minced
Dash dried oregano
Salt
Freshly ground pepper

1 In medium bowl, combine beans, celery and onion; set aside.

2 In small saucepan, whisk together oil, vinegar, garlic and oregano; heat dressing over medium heat just until hot. Toss with bean mixture. Add salt and pepper to taste.

4 (½-cup) servings

ASPARAGUS SALAD

Mimi Cruse
Westlake, Ohio

2 lb. fresh asparagus, stems removed
¾ cup olive oil
¼ cup red wine vinegar
½ cup chopped fresh basil
1½ tablespoons Dijon mustard
½ cup crumbled feta cheese
½ cup chopped walnuts
½ cup sun-dried tomatoes in oil, drained, chopped

1 In large pot with steamer insert, steam asparagus until tender but crisp. Refresh under cold water; drain. Place on large serving platter in a single layer.

2 In medium bowl, whisk together oil, vinegar, basil and mustard. Just before serving, toss with asparagus, cheese, walnuts and tomatoes. Serve over greens, if desired.

6 to 8 servings

TUNA SALAD

Lynne Hudson
Chesapeake, Virginia

1 (6-oz.) can tuna in spring water, drained

1/3 cup chopped walnuts

1/3 cup finely diced celery

1/3 cup finely diced apple (such as Gala)

1/8 teaspoon celery salt

1/3 to 1/2 cup mayonnaise

In small bowl, combine tuna, walnuts, celery, apple and celery salt. Add mayonnaise 1 tablespoon at a time until of desired consistency. Refrigerate until ready to serve.

2 (3/4-cup) servings

ZUCCHINI SOUP

Rose Sienkiewicz
Chandler, Arizona

4 lb zucchini, cut into 1-inch pieces

3 (14 1/2-oz.) cans reduced-sodium chicken broth

3 teaspoons salt

1 1/2 teaspoon onion powder

1 1/2 teaspoon garlic powder

1/4 teaspoon freshly ground white pepper

1 1/4 cups reduced-fat cottage cheese

1 cup milk

1/4 cup chopped chives

1 In large pot, combine zucchini, broth, salt, onion powder, garlic powder, and pepper. Bring to a boil over medium-high heat. Simmer, covered, 5 minutes or until zucchini is tender. Remove from heat. Puree with hand blender.

2 In medium bowl, combine cottage cheese and milk; puree with hand blender 45 seconds or until smooth and creamy. Add to zucchini mixture; mix until well combined.

3 Before serving, briefly return soup to heat to warm. Garnish with chives. Season with additional salt and pepper, if desired.

12 servings

MINESTRONE

Carol Jackson
Broken Arrow, Oklahoma

2 tablespoons olive oil

1 cup coarsely chopped onion

2 garlic gloves, minced

1/2 cup thickly sliced carrots

1/2 cup thinly sliced celery

1/2 cup chopped green bell pepper

4 cups chicken or vegetable stock

1 (28-oz.) can Italian plum tomatoes, undrained

1 medium zucchini, unpeeled, cut into small cubes

1 cup green beans, cut into 1-inch pieces

2 tablespoons chopped fresh basil

1 tablespoon chopped oregano

1/2 teaspoon salt

1/2 teaspoon freshly ground pepper

1/2 cup elbow macaroni

1 (15-oz.) can garbanzo beans, drained

1 (15-oz.) can red kidney beans, drained

1 cup finely sliced cabbage

1/4 cup chopped fresh parsley

1/4 cup freshly grated Parmesan cheese (1 oz.)

1 In large pot, heat oil over medium-high heat until hot. Add onion, garlic, carrots, celery and bell pepper; sauté 3 to 5 minutes or until onion is tender. Add broth, tomatoes, zucchini, green beans, basil, oregano, salt and pepper; mix gently. Bring to a boil; reduce heat to low. Cover; simmer 40 minutes, stirring occasionally.

2 Add macaroni, garbanzo beans, kidney beans and cabbage. Cover; simmer an additional 15 minutes or until macaroni and cabbage are tender, stirring occasionally. (If soup is too thick, add additional broth or water.) Garnish with parsley and cheese.

8 servings

SESAME SHRIMP SOBA SALAD

Jeannine LeVigne
Dryden, Maine

DRESSING

¼ cup dried shiitake mushrooms

1 tablespoon minced fresh ginger

2 tablespoons dark sesame oil

2 tablespoons Thai lemon grass dressing*

2 tablespoons rice vinegar

1 tablespoon hot chili sauce

1 teaspoon honey

SALAD

8 oz. soba noodles**

2 cups broccoli florets

1 large carrot, sliced

1 tablespoon vegetable oil

1 lb. shelled, deveined uncooked medium shrimp

2 garlic cloves, minced

2 cups chopped bok choy

6 green onions, sliced

¼ cup sesame seeds

TOPPING

2 tablespoons sesame seeds

2 teaspoons kosher (coarse) salt

1 Place mushrooms in medium bowl; cover with boiling water. Let stand 15 minutes. Drain mushrooms, reserving ¼ cup liquid. In food processor, combine mushrooms with reserved liquid, ginger, sesame oil, lemon grass dressing, rice vinegar, chili sauce and honey; pulse just until mushrooms are finely chopped. Set aside.

2 Cook noodles in boiling salted water 7 to 8 minutes or until al dente, adding broccoli and carrot during last minute of cooking time. Drain; rinse with cold water to cool. Place in large bowl; set aside.

3 In large skillet, heat oil over medium heat until hot. Add shrimp and garlic; sauté until shrimp turn pink. Add to noodle mixture. Add bok choy, onions and sesame seeds; toss to combine.

4 Pour dressing over noodle mixture; toss lightly.

5 In a small bowl, combine sesame seeds and kosher salt; mix well. Sprinkle over salad. Serve chilled or at room temperature.

TIPS *One tablespoon lemon juice can be substituted for the lemon grass dressing.

**Soba noodles are Japanese buckwheat noodles found in specialty food shops or health food stores.

10 servings

SESAME SHRIMP SOBA SALAD

SALAD WITH AVOCADO DRESSING

Elizabeth Long
West Hollywood, California

SALAD

1 (6.5-oz.) jar marinated artichoke hearts

6 cups mixed salad greens

1 (15-oz.) can Mandarin oranges, drained

1 (8-oz.) can water chestnuts, drained, sliced

DRESSING

1 avocado

1/4 cup mayonnaise

1/4 cup fresh orange juice

1/4 cup fresh lemon juice

1/4 cup finely chopped radishes

1/4 cup finely chopped green onions

1/4 cup finely chopped seeded cucumber

1 Drain artichoke hearts, reserving 2 tablespoons liquid.

2 In food processor or blender, combine avocado, mayonnaise, orange juice, lemon juice and reserved liquid from artichoke hearts; process until pureed. Add radishes, onions and cucumber; process until smooth. Refrigerate 1 hour.

3 In large bowl, combine greens, oranges, water chestnuts and artichoke hearts; toss. Drizzle with avocado dressing;* toss.

TIP *Any remaining avocado dressing can be covered and refrigerated up to 4 days.

6 servings

PESTO CHICKEN SALAD

Barbara Williams
Milwaukee, Wisconsin

PESTO

1 cup chopped fresh basil

1/2 cup chopped fresh parsley

1 tablespoon peanuts

4 medium garlic cloves

1/4 cup olive oil

1/2 cup freshly grated Parmesan cheese (2 oz.)

1/4 teaspoon salt

1/4 teaspoon freshly ground pepper

SALAD

2 (5- to 6-oz.) boneless skinless chicken breast halves, pounded flat

1/2 cup plus 1 tablespoon olive oil

4 cups mixed salad greens

1/4 cup balsamic vinegar

1 Heat broiler. In blender or food processor, combine basil, parsley, peanuts, garlic and enough oil to allow ingredients to process. Process until smooth. Pour into small bowl; stir in cheese, salt and pepper. In another small bowl, reserve 2 tablespoons pesto.

2 Drizzle chicken with 1 tablespoon oil. Brush one side with 1 tablespoon reserved pesto. Place pesto side up on broiler pan. Broil 4 to 6 minutes; turn. Brush plain side with remaining 1 tablespoon reserved pesto. Broil an additional 4 to 6 minutes or until chicken is no longer pink in center. Cut chicken into strips. Place on greens.

3 In small bowl, whisk together 1 tablespoon pesto, 1/2 cup olive oil and vinegar. Pour over greens. Refrigerate or freeze remaining pesto for another use.

4 servings

ITALIAN GARDEN PASTA SALAD

Mari Younkin
Colorado Springs, Colorado

PASTA

1 (1-lb.) pkg. penne

$\frac{1}{2}$ cup cubed Colby cheese

$\frac{1}{2}$ cup cubed hot pepper cheese

$\frac{1}{2}$ cup cubed Provolone cheese

$\frac{1}{2}$ cup julienned Genoa salami

2 plum tomatoes, diced

$\frac{1}{2}$ cup diced red bell pepper

$\frac{1}{2}$ cup pitted ripe olives

$\frac{1}{2}$ cup sliced red onion

$\frac{1}{2}$ cup broccoli florets

$\frac{1}{4}$ cup chopped celery

1 (6.5-oz.) jar marinated artichokes, undrained

$\frac{1}{4}$ cup chopped sun-dried tomatoes, packed in oil and herbs

DRESSING

1$\frac{1}{2}$ cups Italian dressing

2 tablespoons extra-virgin olive oil

1 tablespoon balsamic vinegar

2 garlic cloves, minced

2 tablespoons chopped fresh parsley

1 tablespoon chopped fresh basil or $\frac{1}{2}$ teaspoon dried

1 tablespoon chopped fresh oregano or $\frac{1}{2}$ teaspoon dried

$\frac{1}{2}$ teaspoon salt

$\frac{1}{2}$ teaspoon freshly ground pepper

1 Cook penne according to package directions.

2 In medium bowl, whisk together Italian dressing, olive oil, vinegar, garlic, parsley, basil and oregano.

3 In large bowl, combine penne, cheeses, salami, plum tomatoes, bell pepper, olives, onion, broccoli, celery, artichokes and sun-dried tomatoes. Pour dressing over penne mixture; toss well. Season with salt and pepper. Refrigerate overnight.

4 Before serving, toss pasta. Sprinkle with freshly grated Parmesan cheese, if desired.

8 (1$\frac{1}{2}$-cup) servings

SIMPLE SALAD IN JICAMA BOWL

Denise Spielman
San Francisco, California

VINAIGRETTE

1 to 1$\frac{1}{2}$ garlic cloves, minced

1 tablespoon minced shallot

1 teaspoon Dijon mustard

$\frac{1}{8}$ cup red wine vinegar

$\frac{1}{2}$ teaspoon salt

$\frac{1}{8}$ teaspoon freshly ground pepper

$\frac{1}{4}$ cup vegetable oil

SALAD

8 cups mesclun

2 jicamas, halved, hollowed*

$\frac{1}{2}$ cup pine nuts

1 In small bowl, combine garlic, shallot, mustard, vinegar, salt and pepper; whisk to mix well. Gradually whisk in oil.

2 In large bowl, lightly toss mesclun with vinaigrette; place 2 cups salad in each hollow jicama. Sprinkle with pine nuts.

TIP *Use a melon baller to hollow jicamas to between $\frac{1}{8}$- and $\frac{1}{4}$-inch thickness.

4 servings

SQUASH AND ROASTED CORN CHOWDER

SQUASH AND ROASTED CORN CHOWDER

Denise Spielman
San Francisco, California

3 ears corn

1 large red bell pepper

1 to 2 slices bacon, cut into $\frac{1}{4}$-inch strips

1 tablespoon butter

1 medium onion, diced

1$\frac{1}{2}$ tablespoons all-purpose flour

2$\frac{1}{4}$ cups chicken stock

1 russet potato, diced

$\frac{3}{4}$ cup half-and-half

1 small butternut squash, seeded, diced (about 4 cups)

Salt

Freshly ground pepper

1 Place corn on gas grill on medium heat or on charcoal grill 4 to 6 inches from medium coals. Cook 15 minutes or until slightly charred and crisp-tender, turning frequently. Cut kernels from cob; reserve. Grill bell pepper until blackened on all sides. Place in resealable plastic bag. Seal; let rest 10 minutes. Peel, seed and chop bell pepper.

2 In 3-quart saucepan, sauté bacon over medium-high heat about 4 minutes or just until crisp. Add butter. When butter is melted, add onion; sauté 10 minutes or until onion is tender and transparent. Add flour; cook 4 to 5 minutes. Slowly add stock, stirring constantly. Add potato; simmer 10 minutes or until potato is tender. Add corn, bell pepper and half-and-half. Simmer until mixture is slightly thickened, about 20 minutes. During last 10 minutes of cooking time, add squash.

3 Remove from heat. Season soup with salt and pepper. Garnish with cilantro, if desired.

4($\frac{1}{2}$-cup) servings

CARROT SOUP

Wallace Light
Sunnyvale, California

2 tablespoons reduced-fat margarine

2 garlic cloves, chopped

1 onion, chopped

6 medium carrots, sliced

2 medium potatoes, cut into 1-inch cubes

2 ribs celery, diced

5 sprigs cilantro

1 bay leaf

$\frac{1}{2}$ teaspoon dried thyme

Freshly ground pepper

6 cups chicken stock

1 tablespoon sherry

1 In large saucepan, melt margarine over medium-high heat. Add garlic and onion; sauté about 5 minutes or until lightly browned. Add carrots, potatoes, celery, cilantro, bay leaf, thyme, pepper, broth and sherry. Bring to a boil. Reduce heat to low; cover and simmer 20 minutes or until vegetables are tender. Remove and discard bay leaf. Cool slightly.

2 In blender or food processor, puree vegetables and some of the cooking liquid. Combine pureed vegetable mixture with remaining liquid. Return to saucepan; bring to a simmer over medium heat. Serve hot.

6 (1$\frac{2}{3}$-cup) servings

SPINACH SOUP WITH CHEESE FOAM

Elizabeth Long
West Hollywood, California

3 cups chicken stock

1 cup sour cream

2 teaspoons cornstarch

1 (10-oz.) pkg. frozen spinach, thawed, squeezed dry, chopped

2 egg yolks

1/2 cup whipping cream

1/2 teaspoon salt

1/2 teaspoon freshly ground pepper

1/2 teaspoon grated nutmeg

TOPPING

1/2 cup whipping cream

1/2 cup grated Gruyère cheese (2 oz.)

1 Heat broiler. In blender, puree stock, sour cream and cornstarch. Pour into medium saucepan; add spinach. Bring to a simmer over medium heat.

2 Meanwhile, in blender, combine egg yolks, 1/2 cup whipping cream, salt, pepper and nutmeg; blend well. Add to spinach mixture. Heat over low heat just until hot, being careful not to boil.

3 To make topping, in small bowl, beat 1/2 cup whipping cream until soft peaks form. Stir in cheese.

4 To serve, pour soup into individual oven-proof soup bowls. Spoon cheese mixture over soup. Broil 4 to 6 inches from heat until cheese melts and is golden brown.

6 servings

MANDARIN ORANGE NUT SALAD

Kyra Taylor
Dexter, Missouri

VINAIGRETTE

1/3 cup canola oil

2 tablespoons red wine vinegar

1 teaspoon Dijon mustard

SALAD

1/2 head lettuce, torn into pieces

3 carrots, peeled, sliced

1 (10-oz.) can Mandarin orange slices, drained

1 cup peas

1/2 cup sliced or slivered almonds

1/2 cup salted cashews

2 cups grated sharp cheddar cheese (8 oz.)

1 In small bowl, whisk together oil, vinegar and mustard.

2 In large bowl, combine lettuce, carrots, oranges, peas, almonds and cashews; toss. Pour vinaigrette over salad; toss. Top with cheese.

5 servings

TEXAS CAVIAR SALAD

Mary Jeans
Blackwell, Oklahoma

2 (14-oz.) cans black-eyed peas, drained

1 (15 1/2-oz.) can white hominy, drained

4 green onions, chopped

2 medium tomatoes, chopped

2 garlic cloves, minced

1 medium green bell pepper, chopped

1 jalapeño chile, chopped

1/2 cup chopped onion

1/2 cup chopped fresh parsley

1 (8-oz.) bottle Italian dressing

1 In large bowl, combine peas, hominy, onions, tomatoes, garlic, bell pepper, chile, onion and parsley; mix well. Pour dressing over vegetables; toss.

2 Cover; refrigerate 2 hours.

8 servings

FRUIT-NUT SALAD WITH CURRY VINAIGRETTE

Lori Kennison
Jacksonville, Florida

DRESSING

⅓ cup vegetable oil

⅓ cup white vinegar

1 garlic clove, minced

2 tablespoons packed brown sugar

2 tablespoons minced fresh chives

1 tablespoon curry powder

1 teaspoon low-sodium soy sauce

SALAD

1 head iceberg lettuce, torn into pieces

1 cup spinach, stems removed, torn into pieces

1 cup halved seedless red and green grapes

1 avocado, diced

1 (11-oz.) can Mandarin oranges, chilled, drained

½ cup slivered almonds, toasted*

1 In medium bowl, combine oil, vinegar, garlic, brown sugar, chives, curry powder and soy sauce; mix until brown sugar is dissolved.

2 In large bowl, combine lettuce, spinach, grapes, avocado, oranges and almonds. Toss with vinaigrette; place in serving bowl.

TIP *To toast almonds, spread in large skillet. Cook over medium-high heat about 5 minutes or until lightly browned. Cool.

6 to 8 servings

SAFFRON-SCENTED CHOWDER

William Wortman Jr.
Cornelious, North Carolina

3 tablespoons butter

1 leek, chopped

1 small onion, chopped

½ fennel bulb, fronds removed, chopped

3 garlic cloves, minced

½ teaspoon dried thyme

¼ teaspoon saffron

3 cups fish stock*

½ cup dry white wine

1 lb. potatoes, cubed (about 2 cups)

¼ cup nonfat milk

⅛ teaspoon salt

⅛ teaspoon freshly ground pepper

Fresh basil

1 In large skillet, melt butter over medium-high heat. Add leek, onion, fennel and garlic; sauté 5 minutes or until tender. Stir in thyme, saffron, stock, wine and potatoes; bring to a boil.

2 Reduce heat to medium-low; simmer 15 minutes or until potatoes are tender. Stir in milk, salt and pepper. Increase heat to medium-high; bring to a boil. Pour into soup bowls; garnish with basil.

TIP *Fish bouillon or canned chicken broth can be substituted. If used, omit salt.

About 4 (1¼-cup) servings

PASTA AND SAUSAGE SOUP

Vonda Baker
Beebe, Arkansas

1 lb. Italian sausage, cut into 1-inch pieces

1/2 medium onion, chopped

1/2 medium bell pepper, cut into strips

2 (14 1/2-oz.) cans reduced-sodium chicken broth

1 (14.5-oz.) can diced tomatoes with juice

1 cup farfalle (bow-tie pasta)

1 1/2 teaspoons Worcestershire sauce

1 1/2 teaspoons sugar

1/2 teaspoon dried thyme

1/2 teaspoon dried basil

1/2 teaspoon salt

1/8 teaspoon garlic powder

1 In Dutch oven or large pot, cook sausage, onion and bell pepper over medium-high heat 10 minutes or until sausage is browned.

2 Add broth, tomatoes, pasta, Worcestershire sauce, sugar, thyme, basil, salt and garlic powder; simmer, uncovered, 15 minutes or until pasta is tender.

6 servings

MY FAVORITE CABBAGE SALAD

Bonnie Bowers
Volcano, California

SALAD

1 avocado, halved, diced

Fresh lemon juice

Salt

Freshly ground pepper

1/2 medium head cabbage, shredded (6 cups)

3 green onions, chopped

1 rib celery, diced

1 cup seeded diced tomato

1/2 yellow bell pepper, diced

DRESSING

1 tablespoon balsamic vinegar

1 tablespoon cider vinegar

1 teaspoon Dijon mustard

2 garlic cloves

1/4 teaspoon salt

1/8 teaspoon freshly ground pepper

1/8 teaspoon onion powder

1/2 cup olive oil

1 Place avocado in large bowl; sprinkle lemon juice over to coat. Season with salt and pepper. Add cabbage, onions, celery, tomato and bell pepper; toss.

2 In food processor or blender, combine balsamic vinegar, cider vinegar, mustard, garlic, salt, pepper and onion powder; process until well combined. Slowly add in oil; process until smooth. Toss salad with dressing.

7 servings

MY FAVORITE CABBAGE SALAD

CRAB AND SHRIMP BISQUE

Gloria Dawson
Everett, Washington

¼ cup unsalted butter

¼ cup plus 2 tablespoons all-purpose flour

1 (14½-oz.) can reduced-sodium chicken broth

2 cups half-and-half

⅛ teaspoon sweet paprika

⅛ teaspoon mace

2 tablespoons finely minced onion

2 tablespoons minced fresh parsley

3 tablespoons dry white wine

8 oz. canned crabmeat, undrained

8 oz. shelled, deveined uncooked bay shrimp

1 In large saucepan, melt butter over medium heat. Stir in ¼ cup flour; cook 5 minutes. Slowly whisk in broth, half-and-half, paprika, mace, onion and parsley. Reduce heat to low; simmer 10 minutes or until mixture thickens, being careful not to boil mixture.

2 Meanwhile, in small bowl, combine wine and 2 tablespoons flour. Whisk in 1 cup warm half-and-half mixture; add to wine mixture, whisking until smooth. Add crabmeat with liquid and shrimp; simmer over low heat 15 minutes. Garnish with freshly chopped chives.

6 servings

ROMAINE AND CUCUMBER SALAD WITH GARLIC VINAIGRETTE

Fred Schmidtke
Wake Forest, North Carolina

2 garlic cloves, minced

½ teaspoon salt

2 tablespoons white wine vinegar

⅛ teaspoon freshly ground pepper

⅓ cup olive oil

1 head romaine lettuce, torn into bite-size pieces (about 8 cups)

1 cucumber, halved lengthwise, seeded, sliced (about 3 cups)

In small bowl, mash garlic and salt with fork. In large bowl, whisk together vinegar, garlic mixture and pepper. Gradually whisk in oil. Add lettuce and cucumber; toss.

8 servings

JOANNA'S SIGNATURE SALAD

Joanna Henry
Houston, Texas

6 cups spinach, stems removed, torn into bite-size pieces

1 avocado, cubed

8 mushrooms, quartered

8 medium to large strawberries, hulled, quartered

1 red grapefruit, sectioned

¼ cup slivered almonds, toasted*

½ cup poppy seed dressing

Place spinach in large bowl. Arrange avocado, mushrooms, strawberries and grapefruit over spinach. Sprinkle with almonds. Serve with dressing.

TIP *To toast almonds, spread in large skillet. Cook over medium-high heat about 5 minutes or until lightly browned. Cool.

4 (2½-cup) servings

CRUNCHY-MUNCHY CHICKEN SALAD

Cecelia Rooney
Point Pleasant, New Jersey

1/2 cup coarsely chopped walnuts

1/2 cup sesame seeds

2 cups diced cooked chicken

1/2 cup diced celery

1/4 cup finely chopped onion

1 (8-oz.) can sliced water chestnuts, drained

2/3 cup mayonnaise

1 to 2 tablespoons low-sodium soy sauce

Salt

1/8 teaspoon freshly ground pepper

1 Heat oven to 350°F. Place walnuts and sesame seeds in shallow baking pan; toast 8 to 10 minutes. Set aside to cool.

2 In medium bowl, combine chicken, celery, onion and water chestnuts. Stir in walnuts and sesame seeds.

3 In small bowl, combine mayonnaise and soy sauce; mix well. Pour over chicken mixture; toss thoroughly. Season with salt and pepper. Serve chilled on lettuce leaves.

4 1/2 cups

CHICKEN CONFETTI SALAD

Rosemary Siewert
Apple Valley, Minnesota

DRESSING

1 1/2 cups mayonnaise

3/4 cup freshly grated Parmesan cheese (3 oz.)

2 tablespoons whole milk

2 tablespoons sugar

1 teaspoon freshly ground pepper

SALAD

1 head cauliflower, cut into bite-size pieces

1 cup broccoli, cut into bite-size pieces

1 head lettuce, cut into bite-size pieces (about 8 cups)

1 sweet onion, sliced

1 red bell pepper, chopped

3/4 lb. bacon, cooked, crumbled

2 cups cooked diced chicken

1 In medium bowl, mix together mayonnaise, cheese, milk, sugar and pepper.

2 In large saucepan, bring 1 quart water to a boil over medium-high heat. Add cauliflower and broccoli; cook 2 minutes; Drain; place under cold running water to stop cooking. Cool.

3 In large bowl, combine cauliflower, broccoli, lettuce, onion, bell pepper, bacon and chicken. Cover; refrigerate 1 hour. Toss with dressing.

6 to 8 servings

LENTIL TOMATO SOUP

Joan Deady
San Francisco, California

5 cups water

2 cups lentils

2 tablespoons olive oil

3 ribs celery, thinly sliced

1 medium onion, chopped

3 garlic cloves, minced

3 carrots, cut into $\frac{1}{4}$ inch thick rounds

1 (28-oz.) can tomatoes

2 cups chicken stock

2 tablespoons wine vinegar

$\frac{1}{2}$ teaspoon Worcestershire sauce

$\frac{1}{8}$ teaspoon hot pepper sauce

2 tablespoons chopped fresh thyme

3 oz. feta cheese

1 Bring water to a boil in large pot over medium-high heat; add lentils. Simmer, covered, 30 minutes or until lentils are soft, stirring occasionally. Drain and rinse.

2 In large saucepan, heat olive oil over medium-high heat until hot. Add celery, onion and garlic; sauté 10 minutes or until celery is tender. Add carrots, tomatoes, broth, vinegar, Worcestershire sauce, hot pepper sauce and thyme. Cover; simmer 15 minutes. Add lentils.

3 In blender or food processor, puree soup in batches. To serve, top with cheese.

16 (1-cup) servings

TRI-COLOR VEGETABLE COUSCOUS SALAD

Joan Deady
San Francisco, California

1 cup water

1 cup reduced-sodium vegetable broth

1 cup couscous

3 tablespoons olive oil

1 small zucchini, cut into $\frac{1}{2}$-inch pieces

1 small red bell pepper, chopped

6 green onions, white parts only, chopped

2 cloves garlic, minced

1 (16-ounce) can garbonzo beans, drained

1 medium tomato, chopped

1 pickled pepperoncini, diced

$\frac{1}{4}$ cup fresh lemon juice

1 cup chopped fresh cilantro

$\frac{1}{2}$ teaspoon cumin

1 Bring water to a boil in large pot over medium-high heat. Add broth and couscous; turn off heat. Let stand, covered, 5 to 10 minutes or until all liquid is dissolved, stirring occasionally. Place couscous in large bowl.

2 Heat oil in large skillet over medium-high heat until hot. Add zucchini, pepper, green onions and garlic; sauté 10 minutes or until vegetables are tender, stirring frequently. Add vegetables to couscous; toss. Add beans, tomato, pepperoncini, lemon juice, $\frac{3}{4}$ cup of the cilantro and cumin; toss. Garnish with remaining $\frac{1}{4}$ cup cilantro.

6 to 8 servings

BACON-CABBAGE SOUP

Dell Watts
Rock Island, Illinois

8 slices bacon, cut into 1-inch pieces

¼ cup chopped onion

¼ cup chopped celery

3 cups reduced-sodium beef broth

5 tomatoes, coarsely chopped

1 tablespoon Worcestershire sauce

½ teaspoon garlic salt

½ teaspoon dried parsley

¼ teaspoon dried thyme

¼ teaspoon freshly ground pepper

Dash hot pepper sauce

2½ cups chopped cabbage

1 In large nonreactive Dutch oven or saucepan, cook bacon over medium heat until crisp. Remove bacon and all but 1 tablespoon of the drippings. Drain bacon on paper towels.

2 Add onion and celery to Dutch oven; sauté 5 to 7 minutes or until onion is transparent, stirring frequently. Add broth, tomatoes, Worcestershire sauce, garlic salt, parsley, thyme, pepper and hot pepper sauce; bring to a boil. Reduce heat to low; simmer, uncovered, 25 minutes.

3 Add cabbage; cook 10 minutes. Top each serving with bacon.

4 (1⅓-cup) servings

RED POTATO SALAD WITH CHARDONNAY VINAIGRETTE

Joan Deady
San Francisco, California

3 lb. small red potatoes

3 carrots, shredded

3 ribs celery, diced

3 green onions, chopped

1 shallot, diced

1 (6-oz.) jar marinated artichoke hearts, drained

VINAIGRETTE

¼ cup Chardonnay

3 tablespoons white wine vinegar

2 tablespoons chopped fresh parsley

1 teaspoon ground fennel

1 tablespoon dried dill weed

¼ teaspoon freshly ground pepper

1 Fill large pot half-full with water; add potatoes. Bring to a boil over medium heat. Boil, covered, 20 minutes or until cooked through. Drain and rinse under cold water; cool slightly. Cut into bite-size pieces.

2 Meanwhile, in large bowl, combine carrots, celery, green onion, shallot and artichoke hearts; mix well. In small bowl, combine Chardonnay, vinegar, parsley, fennel, dill and pepper; mix well.

3 Add slightly warm potatoes to carrot mixture; mix to combine. Toss with vinaigrette. Refrigerate 1 hour.

6 to 8 servings

STRAWBERRY & SPINACH SALAD WITH POPPY SEED DRESSING

William Maue
Manistee, Michigan

SALAD

1 large bunch fresh spinach, stems removed, torn into bite-size pieces (about 6 cups)

2 cups fresh strawberries, sliced

DRESSING

$1/4$ cup sugar

1 cup vegetable oil

$1/3$ cup white vinegar

1 tablespoon finely chopped red onion

$1^1/2$ tablespoons poppy seeds

1 teaspoon dry mustard

1 teaspoon salt

In large bowl, combine spinach and strawberries; toss. In blender or food processor, combine sugar, oil, vinegar, onion, poppy seeds, mustard and salt; puree until creamy. Serve salad with dressing.

4 servings

HERBED CHICKEN SALAD

Donna Hawbaker
Bella Vista, Arkansas

1 cup sliced ripe olives

1 cup sliced red bell pepper

$1/2$ cup extra-virgin olive oil

$1/3$ cup herb vinegar

$1/3$ cup freshly grated Parmesan cheese

1 teaspoon dry mustard

$1/2$ teaspoon Worcestershire sauce

Freshly ground pepper

2 (4-oz.) boneless skinless chicken breast halves, cooked, cubed (about 2 cups)

$1/2$ head romaine lettuce, torn into bite-size pieces

$1^1/4$ cups seasoned croutons

1 In shallow baking dish or resealable plastic bag, combine olives, bell pepper, oil, vinegar, cheese, mustard, Worcestershire sauce and pepper; mix well. Add chicken; stir to coat. Marinate overnight, turning chicken occasionally.

2 To serve, toss lettuce with marinade. Sprinkle with croutons.

2 to 3 servings

Sides

SCALLOPED TOMATOES

David Heppner
Brandon, Florida

2 tablespoons olive oil

1 medium green bell pepper, cut into ½-inch pieces

1 medium Spanish onion, coarsely chopped

8 cups day-old bread, crust trimmed, toasted, cut into ½-inch cubes

1 (28-oz.) can diced roasted garlic tomatoes, undrained

1 (10-oz.) can diced tomatoes, undrained

½ cup chopped fresh basil

2 teaspoons sugar

½ teaspoon salt

½ teaspoon freshly ground pepper

½ cup freshly grated Parmesan cheese (2 oz.)

2 tablespoons butter, melted

1 Heat oven to 375°F. Spray 11x7-inch pan with nonstick cooking spray. In large skillet, heat oil over medium-high heat until hot. Add bell pepper and onion; sauté 3 to 5 minutes or until tender. Stir in bread; set aside.

2 In medium saucepan, combine tomatoes, basil, sugar, salt and pepper; bring to a boil over medium-high heat. Add tomato mixture to bread mixture; mix well. Place in pan. Sprinkle with cheese; drizzle with butter.

3 Bake 35 minutes or until lightly browned. Cool on wire rack 10 to 15 minutes before cutting.

6 to 8 servings

SKILLET CABBAGE

Bonnie Bowers
Volcano, California

1 tablespoon bacon drippings*

1 lb. cabbage, chopped (about ½ medium head)

3 ribs celery, chopped

1 large tomato, seeded, chopped

1 medium onion, chopped

1 bell pepper, chopped

1 teaspoon salt

¼ teaspoon freshly ground pepper

In large skillet, melt bacon drippings over medium heat. Add cabbage, celery, tomato, onion, bell pepper, salt and pepper. Cook 5 to 8 minutes or until cabbage is wilted but still crisp.

TIP *If bacon drippings are unavailable, use olive oil.

6 servings

CORN CUSTARD

Richard Rands
Woodland Hills, California

1 tablespoon butter

1 ear corn, cooked

1 egg

½ cup half-and-half

1 tablespoon chopped red bell pepper

1 tablespoon minced green onion tops

1 Heat oven to 350°F. Butter 2 (6-oz.) ramekins. Cut corn from cobs. Scrape cobs with back of knife to extract as much liquid as possible. Set aside.

2 In medium bowl, whisk together egg and half-and-half until blended. Add corn, corn liquid, bell pepper and green onion tops; mix well. Pour into ramekins. Dot mixture with remaining butter. Bake 45 minutes or until custard is set.

2 servings

PIEROGIES

Rosemary Siewert
Apple Valley, Minnesota

DOUGH

2 cups all-purpose flour

1 teaspoon salt

1 egg

1 cup cold mashed potatoes

$\frac{1}{2}$ cup water

FILLING

2 tablespoons sour cream

1 tablespoon cottage cheese

1 egg

$\frac{1}{2}$ teaspoon salt

$\frac{1}{4}$ teaspoon freshly ground pepper

1 tablespoon olive oil

$\frac{1}{2}$ onion, diced

1 tablespoon butter

1 Line baking sheet with parchment paper. In large bowl, combine flour and 1 teaspoon salt; mix well. Add 1 egg, $\frac{1}{2}$ cup of the mashed potatoes and enough water to make a medium-soft dough. Knead on lightly floured surface until smooth. Cover; let stand 10 minutes.

2 In medium bowl, combine remaining 1 cup mashed potatoes, sour cream, cottage cheese, 1 egg, $\frac{1}{2}$ teaspoon salt and pepper. In medium skillet, heat oil over medium heat until hot. Add onion; sauté 3 to 5 minutes or until transparent. Add potato mixture; cook 3 to 5 minutes or until thick, stirring constantly.

3 Roll dough into round, $\frac{1}{16}$-inch-thick. Cut into circles with $2\frac{1}{2}$- to 3-inch cookie cutter. Place 1 teaspoon filling on each circle; fold over and press edges to seal. Place on baking sheet. (*Pierogies may be frozen at this point and placed in freezer bag until ready to use.*)

4 Bring large pot of salted water to a boil over high heat. Reduce heat to medium. Add 5 to 6 pierogies; cook in simmering water 3 to 5 minutes. With slotted spoon, remove from water. Melt butter in medium saucepan over medium-low heat. Add cooked pierogies; cook 10 minutes or until light brown, turning once. Repeat with remaining pierogies.

12 pierogies

RISOTTO

Fred Schmidtke
Wake Forest, North Carolina

$4\frac{1}{2}$ cups beef stock

2 cups water

$\frac{1}{2}$ cup dry white wine

2 tablespoons olive oil

1 medium yellow onion, chopped

2 garlic cloves, crushed

2 cups arborio rice

$\frac{1}{2}$ cup freshly grated Parmesan cheese (2 oz.)

$\frac{1}{4}$ cup chopped fresh parsley

$\frac{1}{2}$ teaspoon salt

$\frac{1}{4}$ teaspoon freshly ground pepper

1 In large saucepan, bring stock, water and wine to a simmer over medium-high heat. Reduce heat to medium-low.

2 Meanwhile, heat oil in another large saucepan over medium heat until hot. Add onion and garlic; sauté 3 minutes. Reduce heat to medium-low. Add rice; stir to coat all grains with oil. Cook 5 to 7 minutes, stirring constantly.

3 Add 1 cup stock mixture; cook until all liquid has been absorbed, stirring constantly. Adjust heat as necessary to keep rice mixture simmering. Continue to add stock mixture $\frac{1}{2}$ cup at a time, cooking and stirring constantly. Cook 25 minutes, adding all but 1 cup of the stock mixture and cooking until stock mixture is absorbed. Add remaining 1 cup stock mixture; cook 5 minutes. Stir in cheese, parsley, salt and pepper.

6 servings

ASPARAGUS WITH TOASTED ALMONDS AND GARLIC

ASPARAGUS WITH TOASTED ALMONDS AND GARLIC

Fred Schmidtke
Wake Forest, North Carolina

2 lb. thin asparagus

¼ cup olive oil

½ cup slivered almonds

4 garlic cloves, thinly sliced

¼ teaspoon salt

¼ teaspoon freshly ground pepper

2 tablespoons sherry vinegar

2 teaspoons butter

1 In large skillet, bring 1 inch water to a boil. Add asparagus; cook 3 minutes or just until tender and bright green. Drain; pat dry.

2 Dry same skillet. Add oil; heat over high heat until hot. Add almonds; cook 45 seconds, stirring constantly. Add asparagus, garlic, salt and pepper; cook 2 minutes or until garlic and almonds are golden brown, stirring often. Stir in vinegar and butter.

8 servings

AUTUMN BAKED CARROTS

Mary Pieper
Quincy, Illinois

2 medium apples, sliced

½ cup cold water

2 cups cooked sliced carrots

2 tablespoons butter

4 teaspoons sugar

⅛ teaspoon cinnamon

1 Heat oven to 350°F. In small saucepan, combine apples and water. Cover; cook over medium heat 5 minutes or until apples are almost tender. Drain.

2 In 2-quart casserole, combine apples and carrots. Dot with butter; sprinkle with sugar and cinnamon. Bake 30 minutes or until glazed.

4 to 6 servings

EASY HOMEMADE SAUSAGE

Mable Watson
Lenoi, North Carolina

1½ lb. lean ground pork

1 teaspoon dried sage

½ teaspoon dried marjoram

½ teaspoon dried thyme

1 teaspoon salt

½ teaspoon crushed red pepper

¼ teaspoon freshly ground pepper

1 Combine pork, sage, marjoram, thyme, salt, red pepper flakes and pepper in large bowl; mix well. Refrigerate at least 2 hours or up to 24 hours.

2 Divide mixture into 14 portions; shape each portion into patty. In large nonstick skillet, cook patties over medium heat until browned and no longer pink in center, turning once.

14 sausage patties

SOUTHERN CANDIED SWEET POTATOES

Elaine Welsh
Rowlett, Texas

4 medium sweet potatoes

1 cup sugar

1 teaspoon cinnamon

1/2 teaspoon nutmeg

Dash salt

6 tablespoons butter, cut up

1 tablespoon all-purpose flour

1/4 cup water

2 (1/8-inch) slices lemon, seeds removed

1 Heat oven to 400°F. Peel potatoes; cut into 1/2-inch slices. Place in 13x9x-inch pan.

2 Sprinkle potatoes evenly with sugar, cinnamon, nutmeg and salt. Dot with butter; sprinkle with flour. Add water; place lemon slices over top. Cover with foil.

3 Bake 30 minutes, spooning sugar mixture occasionally over potatoes. Remove foil; bake an additional 30 minutes or until potatoes are tender and sugar mixture has become a thick syrup, spooning sugar mixture occasionally over potatoes.

8 servings

SPANISH RICE

Virginia Wittmeier
Rapid City, South Dakota

5 to 6 slices bacon

1 medium onion, chopped

1/2 cup chopped green bell pepper

3/4 cup rice

1 1/2 cups water

2 cups canned diced tomatoes, undrained

1 teaspoon salt

1/8 teaspoon freshly ground pepper

1 Heat oven to 350°F. Dice bacon.

2 In nonreactive Dutch oven or large pot, combine bacon, onion and bell pepper. Cook over medium-high heat 5 to 8 minutes or until bacon is browned and onion is transparent. Add rice; cook until rice begins to brown. Add water; cook 20 to 25 minutes or until rice is tender. Fold in tomatoes with juices, salt and pepper. Pour into 1½-quart casserole. Bake 20 minutes.

4¾ cups

MAQUE CHOUX

Richard Rands
Woodland Hills, California

3 ears corn

2 tablespoons butter

1/4 cup finely chopped onion

1/4 cup finely chopped green bell pepper

1 large tomato, peeled, chopped

1/2 cup chicken stock

1 1/2 teaspoons minced fresh parsley

1/4 teaspoon salt

1/4 teaspoon freshly ground pepper

1 Cut corn from cobs. Scrape cobs with back of knife to extract as much liquid as possible. Set aside.

2 In large saucepan, melt butter over medium-high heat. Add onions and bell pepper; sauté 4 to 5 minutes or until onions are transparent but not brown. Add corn, corn liquid, tomato and broth; simmer, covered, 15 minutes. Stir in parsley, salt and pepper.

4 (1/2-cup) servings

CRISP ROSEMARY POTATOES

Sharon O'Connell
Milwaukee, Wisconsin

7 medium potatoes, unpeeled, cut into bite-size cubes (about 3 cups)

¼ cup olive oil

2 tablespoons butter

1 tablespoon fresh rosemary

1 tablespoon fresh thyme

1 teaspoon freshly ground pepper

½ teaspoon salt

1 Place potatoes in large pot; cover with water. Bring to a boil; partially cover and simmer 25 to 30 minutes or until tender. Drain.

2 In large skillet, heat oil and butter over medium-high heat until bubbly. Add potatoes, rosemary, thyme, pepper and salt. Toss potatoes until well covered with oil and seasonings. Press potatoes, flattening into skillet. Toss potatoes occasionally, flattening after each toss. Cook until evenly browned and crisp.

2 cups

CHEESE-RICE LOAF

Audrey Derr
Valrieo, Florida

1 tablespoon butter

1 cup chopped red bell pepper

⅓ cup chopped shallots

6 oz. chopped fresh mushrooms

¾ cup mayonnaise

4 cups hot cooked rice

1 cup shredded Mexican-blend cheese (4 oz.)

⅔ cup unseasoned bread crumbs

½ teaspoon salt

⅛ teaspoon freshly ground pepper

1 Heat oven to 350°F. Spray 9x5x3-inch loaf pan with nonstick cooking spray.

2 In medium skillet, melt butter over medium heat. Add bell pepper, shallots and mushrooms; cook 6 to 8 minutes or until tender. Remove from heat.

3 In large bowl, combine mayonnaise, rice, cheese, bread crumbs, salt, pepper and bell pepper mixture; mix until well blended. Press mixture into pan. Bake 30 to 35 minutes or until heated through.

4 Cool in pan 5 minutes. Unmold onto serving platter. Garnish with parsley, if desired.

6 to 8 servings

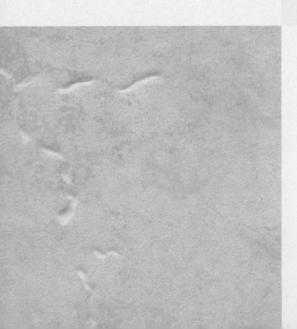

NAPLES TRAIN STATION ROASTED RED PEPPERS

Mike Marshall
Buffalo, New York

4 large red bell peppers

3 tablespoons extra-virgin olive oil

3 tablespoons freshly grated Romano cheese

3 tablespoons bread crumbs

1 tablespoon balsamic vinegar

10 medium basil leaves, thinly sliced

1 Roast peppers on gas grill over high heat or on charcoal grill 4 to 6 inches from hot coals until blackened on all sides. Place peppers in resealable plastic bag; close bag and let stand 15 minutes or until peppers are cool enough to handle. Peel peppers under running water; remove charred skins. Slit peppers open; remove seeds and veins. Cut into quarters.

2 Heat broiler. Place peppers on broiling pan insides up; spray with olive oil. Sprinkle with cheese and bread crumbs. Broil 2 minutes or until cheese bubbles and bread crumbs are toasted. Drizzle with vinegar; sprinkle with basil.

16 appetizers

BLACK BEANS AND RICE

Lisa Imerman
Waterford, Michigan

1 lb. black beans

2 bay leaves

6 garlic cloves

2 to 3 tablespoons olive oil

1 cup diced onion

1 green bell pepper, diced

1 tablespoon white vinegar

2 teaspoons salt

1 tablespoon tomato paste

1 teaspoon cumin

6 cups cooked white rice

1 In medium bowl, soak beans in cold water 2 hours. Drain.

2 In large saucepan, combine beans, bay leaves and 3 garlic cloves. Add enough water to cover beans (about 4 cups). Bring to boil over medium-high heat. Reduce heat to medium; simmer, covered, 2 hours or until beans are tender, adding water as needed to avoid burning beans.

3 Just before beans are done cooking, heat oil in medium skillet over medium-high heat until hot. Add onion, bell pepper, vinegar and remaining 3 garlic cloves; sauté 3 to 5 minutes or until onion is transparent.

4 When beans are tender, remove and discard bay leaves. Add salt, onion mixture, tomato paste and cumin; mix well. (Additional water may be added if mixture is too dry.) Cook 5 minutes or until tomato paste is completely mixed in. Serve over rice.

7 cups

BLACK BEANS AND RICE

EGGPLANT-STUFFED PEPPERS

EGGPLANT-STUFFED PEPPERS

Lorraine Terra
Brooklyn, New York

    2 tablespoons vegetable oil

    1 large eggplant, cut into bite-size pieces

    3 garlic cloves

    1 cup seasoned bread crumbs

    1/2 cup freshly grated Parmesan cheese (2 oz.)

    1/2 cup chopped fresh basil

    1/2 cup chopped fresh parsley

    1/2 teaspoon salt

    1/2 teaspoon freshly ground pepper

    4 red bell peppers, cut lengthwise, seeds removed, parboiled

    8 slices mozzarella cheese

1 Heat oven to 350°F. In large skillet, heat oil over medium-high heat until hot. Add eggplant and garlic; sauté 7 to 10 minutes or until tender. Stir in bread crumbs. Add Parmesan cheese, basil, parsley, salt and pepper.

2 Fill pepper halves halfway with bread crumb mixture. Place 1 slice mozzarella cheese in each pepper; top each with remaining bread crumb mixture. Add 1/2 cup water to 13x9-inch pan; place pepper halves in pan. Bake 1 hour or until peppers are tender and filling is very hot.

8 servings

HEAVENLY CORN PUDDING

Lori Kennison
Jacksonville, Florida

    3 egg whites

    2 cups fresh corn

    1 cup heavy cream

    1/2 teaspoon salt

    1/2 teaspoon freshly ground pepper

    1/4 teaspoon freshly ground nutmeg

    3 eggs, beaten

    1/2 cup grated Swiss cheese (2 oz.)

1 Heat oven to 300°F. Grease 8-inch round cake pan with butter. In small bowl, beat egg whites until stiff peaks form. Set aside.

2 In medium bowl, combine corn, cream, salt, pepper, nutmeg and eggs. Gradually fold in egg whites. Place in pan. Top with cheese. Bake, uncovered 30 minutes. Increase oven temperature to 375°F; bake an additional 10 minutes or until top is golden brown. If desired, top with crumbled bacon and finely chopped chives.

4 to 6 servings

HOPPIN' JOHN

Linda Ferguson
Eustis, Florida

1/4 lb. salt pork, diced

1 medium onion, coarsely chopped

1 1/2 to 2 ribs celery, chopped

1 garlic clove, minced

2 cups water

1 teaspoon salt

1/8 teaspoon hot pepper sauce

1 cup uncooked rice

1 (16-oz.) can black-eyed peas, drained, rinsed

1 In Dutch oven or large pot, fry pork over medium heat until crisp and fat has been rendered. Add onion, celery and garlic; cook until vegetables are tender but not brown. Add water, salt and hot pepper sauce; bring to a boil. Cover. Reduce heat to low; simmer 30 minutes.

2 Stir in rice; cook 20 to 25 minutes or until rice is tender and liquid has been absorbed. Add peas during last 10 minutes of cooking time.

6 servings

CREAMY CORN AND ZUCCHINI

David Heppner
Brandon, Florida

1 (16-oz.) bag frozen corn

3 medium zucchini, sliced 1/8 to 1/4 inch thick

1 cup reduced-fat sour cream (8 oz.)

1 cup reduced-fat cottage cheese

1/2 cup freshly grated Parmesan cheese (2 oz.)

1 teaspoon salt

1/2 teaspoon freshly ground pepper

1 In large saucepan, bring 2/3 cup water to a boil over medium-high heat. Add corn; return to a boil. Reduce heat to medium-low; simmer 2 minutes. Add zucchini; cook 10 minutes or until zucchini is tender. Remove from heat; drain.

2 In medium bowl, combine sour cream, cottage cheese and Parmesan cheese; mix well. Stir into corn mixture. Season with salt and pepper.

8 servings

CRANBERRY-PORT RELISH

Betty L. Nickel
Watsonville, California

3 cups fresh cranberries

1 1/2 cups tawny port

1 1/4 cups sugar

1 cup golden raisins

1 medium onion, finely chopped

2 tablespoons cider vinegar

1 teaspoon ground ginger

1 teaspoon cinnamon

1/2 teaspoon nutmeg

1 In large saucepan, combine cranberries, port, sugar, raisins, onion, vinegar, ginger, cinnamon and nutmeg; mix well. Bring to a boil over medium-high heat, stirring occasionally.

2 Reduce heat to medium-low; simmer, uncovered, 30 minutes or until cranberries have popped and liquid has slightly thickened. Cool to room temperature. Cover and store in refrigerator.

3 1/2 cups

Meats

ORANGE-MARINATED PORK CHOPS

Fia Andersson
Belle Harbor, New York

PORK

4 (1-inch-thick) center-cut pork chops

Freshly ground pepper

$1\frac{1}{2}$ teaspoons butter

$1\frac{1}{2}$ teaspoons olive oil

MARINADE

$\frac{1}{2}$ cup fresh orange juice

2 tablespoons Worcestershire sauce

1 tablespoon low-sodium soy sauce

2 teaspoons honey

1 teaspoon fresh lemon juice

1 Pierce pork slightly with fork; sprinkle with pepper.

2 In small bowl, combine orange juice, Worcestershire sauce, soy sauce, honey and lemon juice. Place pork chops in shallow baking dish; pour marinade over pork. Cover; refrigerate overnight.

3 Remove pork from marinade; discard marinade. In large skillet, heat butter and oil over high heat. When butter is melted, add pork; cook 2 minutes, turning once. Reduce heat to low; cook an additional 10 minutes or until pork is browned and no longer pink in center, turning once. Place pork on plate; cover loosely with foil.

4 Serve with rice. Garnish with one slice of orange, if desired.

4 servings

PHEASANT WITH POMEGRANATE SAUCE

Denise Spielman
San Francisco, California

PHEASANT

2 (4 oz.) boneless skinless breast halves from 1 pheasant

$1\frac{1}{2}$ cups frozen pomegranate juice, thawed

Salt

Freshly ground black pepper

2 tablespoons safflower oil

SAUCE

$\frac{1}{4}$ cup raspberry preserves

$\frac{1}{8}$ cup port

1 teaspoon fresh lemon juice

$\frac{3}{4}$ cup frozen pomegranate juice, thawed

Salt

Ground white pepper

1 Place pheasant in large resealable plastic bag. Add $1\frac{1}{2}$ cups pomegranate juice; seal bag. Marinate in refrigerator at least 4 hours or up to 24 hours, turning frequently.

2 Heat oven to 350°F. Remove pheasants from marinade; pat dry. Discard marinade. Season with salt and black pepper. Brush with oil. In large skillet, sear pheasants on all sides over medium-high heat; transfer to 13x9-inch pan. Bake 40 to 45 minutes or until pheasant thighs are no longer pink in center.

3 In small saucepan, combine preserves, port and lemon juice. Cook over low heat 2 to 3 minutes, stirring constantly. When preserves are melted, stir in $\frac{3}{4}$ cup pomegranate juice; increase heat to medium-high. Cook 10 to 12 minutes or until reduced to sauce consistency. Season with salt and white pepper. Keep warm. Serve pheasants with sauce.

4 servings

STEAK L'MACHA

Lynda Macha
Plainville, Connecticut

1 tablespoon olive oil

1 onion, thinly sliced

1 lb. sliced fresh mushrooms

1 pkg. powdered gravy mix

1 tablespoon Worcestershire sauce

1 tablespoon red wine

$\frac{1}{2}$ teaspoon plus $\frac{1}{8}$ teaspoon freshly ground pepper

1 tablespoon cognac

4 (1-inch-thick) beef tenderloin fillets

$\frac{1}{8}$ teaspoon salt

$\frac{1}{2}$ cup freshly grated Parmesan cheese (2 oz.)

$\frac{1}{4}$ lb. Swiss cheese, sliced

1 In medium skillet, heat oil over medium-high heat until hot. Add onion; sauté 8 to 10 minutes or until onion begins to caramelize. Add mushrooms; cook 5 minutes or until lightly browned.

2 Prepare gravy according to package directions. When simmering, add Worcestershire sauce, wine and $\frac{1}{2}$ teaspoon pepper. Simmer until mixture thickens. Remove from heat; stir in cognac. Set aside.

3 Season fillets on each side with salt and $\frac{1}{8}$ teaspoon pepper. Cook on gas grill over medium heat or on charcoal grill 4 to 6 inches from medium heat 10 minutes, turning once. Place fillets on serving platter; let rest 5 minutes.

4 Heat broiler. Cut fillets into bite-size pieces; place in 1 large or 4 small gratin dishes. Place dish or dishes on baking sheet. Add onions and mushrooms to fillets; top with gravy. Cover with Parmesan cheese and Swiss cheese. Broil 3 to 4 minutes or until cheeses are brown and bubbly.

4 servings

SWEET-TART RIBS

Judi Shadle
Manteo, North Carolina

16 baby back ribs (about 2$\frac{1}{4}$ lbs.)

1 teaspoon garlic salt

1 teaspoon freshly ground pepper

1 teaspoon low-sodium soy sauce

2$\frac{1}{3}$ cups packed brown sugar

1$\frac{1}{4}$ cups ketchup

$\frac{1}{2}$ teaspoon garlic powder

$\frac{1}{2}$ teaspoon instant coffee granules

$\frac{1}{2}$ teaspoon water

1 Heat oven to 475°F. Line 2 (13x9-inch) pans with aluminum foil; spray with nonstick cooking spray. Place ribs in pans; sprinkle with garlic salt, pepper and soy sauce. Bake 5 to 10 minutes or until ribs begin to brown. Remove from oven; set aside. Reduce oven temperature to 350°F.

2 In small bowl, combine brown sugar and ketchup; mix until sugar is no longer dry. Add garlic powder, coffee granules and water; mix until well blended. (If mixture is too tart, add more brown sugar; if too sweet, add more ketchup.) Brush sides and tops of ribs with brown sugar mixture.

3 Bake an additional 45 minutes, basting ribs with brown sugar mixture every 15 minutes. Before final basting, bring remaining mixture to a boil. Serve with ribs.

4 servings

OSSO BUCO WITH GREMOLATA

Fred Schmidtke
Wake Forest, North Carolina

¼ cup butter

6 tablespoons olive oil

4 garlic cloves

2 cups chopped onions

1 cup chopped carrots

1 cup chopped celery

8 (1½- to 2-inch-thick) center-cut veal shanks

Salt

Freshly ground pepper

All-purpose flour

1 cup dry white wine

4 cups beef stock

1¾ cups chopped canned Italian-style tomatoes, undrained

2 bay leaves

2 (3-inch) strips lemon peel

1 teaspoon dried basil

1 teaspoon dried thyme

⅛ teaspoon freshly ground nutmeg

GREMOLATA

½ cup chopped fresh Italian parsley

2 tablespoons grated lemon peel

4 garlic cloves, minced

1 In nonreactive Dutch oven or large pot, heat butter and 2 tablespoons oil over medium-high heat. When butter is melted, add garlic, onions, carrots and celery; sauté 15 minutes or until golden brown. Remove from heat; set aside.

2 Season veal with salt and pepper. Coat with flour; shake off excess. In large skillet, heat remaining ¼ cup oil over high heat until hot. Add veal in batches; cook 8 minutes per batch or until brown on all sides. Place veal on vegetables in Dutch oven.

3 To same large skillet, add wine. Bring to a boil; boil 3 minutes, scraping up any brown bits. Pour wine mixture over veal.

4 Add broth, tomatoes with juices, bay leaves, lemon peel, basil, thyme and nutmeg to veal. Bring to a boil. Reduce heat. Cover; simmer 2 hours or until veal is tender.

5 Just before veal is done, make Gremolata. In small bowl, combine parsley, lemon peel and garlic; mix well. Stir half of Gremolata into veal mixture; simmer 5 minutes to blend flavors. Transfer veal to platter; loosely cover with foil. Boil remaining liquid 20 to 25 minutes or until reduced to about 3½ cups. Season with additional salt and pepper, if desired. Pour over veal; sprinkle with remaining Gremolata.

8 servings

OSSO BUCO WITH GREMOLATA

GRILLED STEAK SALAD

Abeer Suheimat
Grand Prairie, Texas

SEASONING

1 garlic clove, minced

1 teaspoon dried oregano

¼ teaspoon freshly ground pepper

SALAD

1¼ lb. boneless (¾ inch thick) beef top sir-loin steak

Salt

1 teaspoon fresh lemon juice

6 cups mixed salad greens

4 medium plum tomatoes, halved lengthwise, sliced crosswise.

½ cup ranch dressing

1 Heat grill. In small bowl, combine garlic, oregano and pepper. Press evenly onto both sides of steak.

2 Place steak on gas grill over medium-high heat or on charcoal grill 4 to 6 inches from medium-high coals. Grill 16 minutes for medium rare, or until of desired doneness, turning once. Season steak with salt; drizzle with lemon juice. Carve steak crosswise into thin slices.

3 In large bowl, combine greens and tomatoes; toss gently. Arrange steak on top of greens. Serve with dressing.

4 servings

MEXICAN CASSEROLE

Mary Jeans
Blackwell, Oklahoma

1 (10 ¾-oz.) can cream of mushroom soup

⅓ soup can (about 3.5 oz.) water

½ lb. pasteurized process cheese spread, diced

1 (4-oz.) can chopped chiles

2 lb. ground beef

1 medium onion, chopped

1 (10-oz.) can enchilada sauce

1 teaspoon salt

12 corn tortillas, quartered

1 Heat oven to 350°F. In medium saucepan, combine soup, water, cheese and chiles; heat slowly over low heat, stirring occasionally.

2 In large skillet, brown beef and onions over medium-high heat; drain fat. Add enchilada sauce and salt; simmer briefly.

3 Line bottom of 13x9-inch casserole or pan with half of tortillas. Cover with layer of beef, then with layer of soup mixture. Repeat layering once. Bake 40 minutes or until bubbly. If desired, sprinkle with additional cheese before serving.

12 servings

RIGATONI CARBONARA

Priscilla Migliore
Sherman Oaks, California

1 (1-lb.) pkg. rigatoni

2 tablespoons extra-virgin olive oil

$\frac{1}{4}$ lb. aged ham (such as prosciutto), cut into matchstick-size pieces

$\frac{1}{4}$ cup chopped yellow onion

1 garlic clove, minced

$\frac{3}{4}$ cup pasteurized egg substitute

$\frac{1}{2}$ cup grated Romano cheese (2 oz.)

Salt

Freshly ground pepper

$\frac{1}{4}$ cup chopped fresh cilantro

1 Cook rigatoni according to package directions.

2 In large skillet, heat oil over medium heat until hot. Add ham, onion and garlic; sauté 4 to 5 minutes or until onion is transparent. Add rigatoni to ham mixture.

3 In small bowl, combine egg substitute, cheese, salt and pepper; mix well. Add to rigatoni mixture; toss to evenly coat rigatoni. Before serving, sprinkle with cilantro.

4 servings

ARTICHOKE AND PORK SAUTE

William Wortman Jr.
Cornelious, North Carolina

1 cup butter

2 lb. boneless pork loin, cut into $\frac{3}{4}$-inch-thick medallions

3 (9-oz.) pkg. frozen artichoke hearts, thawed

1 lb. unpeeled apple slices ($\frac{1}{4}$ inch thick)

4 green onions, sliced

1$\frac{1}{2}$ tablespoons sage

1 tablespoon minced garlic

$\frac{1}{2}$ cup apple brandy

Chicken stock

Salt

1 In large skillet, melt butter over medium-high heat. Add pork; sauté 5 minutes or until no longer pink in center, turning once. Remove pork from skillet; set aside.

2 In same large skillet, sauté artichoke hearts over medium-high heat 5 minutes or until tender. Add apples, onions, sage, garlic and brandy; toss to combine. Cook 2 to 3 minutes. If mixture is too thick, add enough stock to moisten. Season with salt.

3 Serve pork with artichoke mixture. Garnish with sprig of sage, if desired.

8 servings

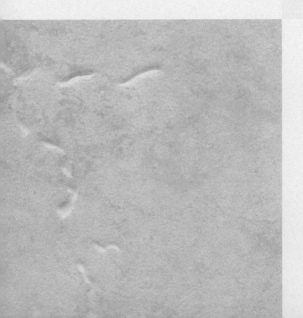

PORK MEDALLIONS WITH GREEN PEPPERCORN SAUCE

PORK MEDALLIONS WITH GREEN PEPPERCORN SAUCE

Beverly Woods
Qunicy, California

PORK

4 (½-lb.) pork tenderloins

1 teaspoon Dijon mustard

⅓ cup olive oil

1 large garlic clove, minced

2 teaspoons minced fresh thyme

2 teaspoons minced fresh rosemary

2 tablespoons fresh lemon juice

Salt

Freshly ground black pepper

SAUCE

1 tablespoon butter

1 shallot, minced

1 carrot, minced

2 tablespoons green peppercorns

1 cup whipping cream

¼ teaspoon salt

Ground white pepper

1 Place pork in 3-quart casserole. Spread mustard over pork; drizzle with olive oil. Sprinkle with garlic, thyme, rosemary and lemon juice. Season with salt and black pepper. Cover; refrigerate overnight.

2 Heat oven to 400°F. Place pork in 13x9-inch pan. Bake 35 to 40 minutes or until internal temperature reaches 155°F. (If desired, broil first to brown.) Remove pork from pan; cover loosely with foil.

3 In same pan, melt butter with pork drippings over medium-high heat. Add shallot and carrot; sauté 3 to 5 minutes or until shallot is tender. Stir in peppercorns; simmer until carrot is tender. Stir in cream; cook 5 to 10 minutes or until sauce is reduced and coats the back of a spoon. Season with ¼ teaspoon salt and white pepper.

4 To serve, slice pork into medallions. Serve with Peppercorn Sauce.

6 servings

OVEN-BRAISED BRISKET WITH ONIONS

Pam Stull
Sunnyvale, California

4 lb. fresh center-cut beef brisket, trimmed

3 medium onions, sliced

¼ cup packed brown sugar

1½ cups red wine (such as Zinfandel)

¼ cup red wine vinegar

2 tablespoons low-sodium soy sauce

2 teaspoons paprika

3 garlic cloves, minced

1 tablespoon cornstarch

1 tablespoon water

Chopped fresh parsley

1 Heat oven to 450°F. Place brisket in large oval roasting pan. Bake, uncovered, 15 to 30 minutes or until top is lightly browned. Turn meat over; bake an additional 5 minutes or until brown. Remove from oven. Reduce oven temperature to 325°F.

2 Arrange onions overlapping on top of brisket. In small bowl, combine brown sugar, wine, vinegar, soy sauce, paprika and garlic; mix well. Pour over brisket. Cover tightly with foil. Bake 3 to 3½ hours or until meat is very tender when pierced with knife.

3 To make gravy, pour brisket juices into medium saucepan. In small bowl, whisk together cornstarch and water; add to brisket juices. Boil over high heat 1 to 2 minutes or until sauce thickens. Serve with brisket. Sprinkle parsley over brisket.

6 to 8 servings

MEDALLIONS OF VEAL TROCADERO

Elizabeth Long
West Hollywood, California

VEAL

4 (4-oz.) veal medallions*

1/2 teaspoon salt

1/2 teaspoon freshly ground pepper

All-purpose flour

2 tablespoons butter

4 slices cooked ham

4 slices Swiss cheese

MUSHROOM SAUCE

1/2 cup butter

2 cups sliced mushrooms

2 tablespoons all-purpose flour

1 cup half-and-half

Salt

Freshly ground pepper

HOLLANDAISE SAUCE

3 egg yolks

2 tablespoons fresh lemon juice

1/4 teaspoon salt

1/2 cup butter, melted

1 Heat broiler. Pound veal medallions fairly thin; season with 1/2 teaspoon each of the salt and pepper. Dredge each medallion in flour; shake off excess. Set aside.

2 In medium skillet, melt 1/2 cup butter over medium-high heat. Add mushrooms; sauté until well cooked. Stir in 2 tablespoons flour and cook 1 to 2 minutes. Stir in half-and-half; bring to a boil, stirring constantly. Boil 2 to 3 minutes to thicken. Add salt and pepper to taste. (*Sauce can be made up to 4 hours ahead. Cover and refrigerate.*)

3 In small bowl, whisk together egg yolks, lemon juice and 1/4 teaspoon salt. Fill bottom of double boiler with water; bring to a simmer. Place egg yolk mixture in top of double boiler; heat over simmering water just until mixture begins to thicken. Slowly whisk in 1/2 cup melted butter. Turn off heat; continue whisking mixture. (If mixture looks as if it will curdle, lift top off double boiler and whisk mixture slightly to cool; return to double boiler.) Set aside.

4 In large skillet, melt 2 tablespoons butter over medium-high heat. Add veal; sauté 4 minutes or until browned, turning once. Place on large baking sheet. Layer each medallion with 1 slice ham and 1 slice cheese; spoon mushroom mixture over medallions. Drizzle medallions with hollandaise sauce. Broil 4 to 6 inches from heat for 2 to 3 minutes or until hollandaise is golden.

TIP *If veal medallions are unavailable, use thinly sliced bone-in veal chops.

4 servings

VEAL SCALOPPINI

Sherry Huff
Sacramento, California

4 veal scallops, halved (about 9 oz.)

8 sage leaves

8 thin slices proscuitto

1/2 teaspoon freshly ground pepper

Dash salt

2 tablespoons olive oil

1/4 cup chopped shallot

2 garlic cloves, minced

1/4 lb. cremini mushrooms, thinly sliced

1/2 cup beef stock

1/2 cup dry white wine

1/4 cup heavy cream

2 oz. blue cheese

2 tablespoons minced Italian parsley

1 Pound veal between pieces of plastic wrap to 1/8 inch. Layer each veal piece with 1 sage leaf and 1 slice prosciutto. Roll up veal, starting with short side; secure with toothpick. Season with pepper and salt.

2 In large skillet, heat oil over high heat until hot. Add shallot and garlic; sauté 3 minutes or until tender. Reduce heat to medium-high. Add veal; sauté 10 minutes or until golden brown. Remove from pan; cover loosely with aluminum foil.

3 Reduce heat to medium. Add mushrooms, stock and wine to skillet; sauté 8 to 10 minutes, stirring occasionally. Add cream and cheese; simmer 10 minutes or until sauce thickens. Remove toothpick from veal. Add veal during last 2 to 3 minutes of cooking time. Sprinkle with parsley.

4 servings

HONEY-GINGERED PORK TENDERLOIN

William Wortman Jr.
Cornelious, North Carolina

1/4 cup honey

1/4 cup low-sodium soy sauce

1/4 cup oyster sauce

2 tablespoons packed brown sugar

1 tablespoon plus 1 teaspoon minced fresh ginger

1 tablespoon minced garlic

1 tablespoon ketchup

1/4 teaspoon onion powder

1/4 teaspoon ground red pepper

1/4 teaspoon cinnamon

2 (11-oz.) pork tenderloins

Fresh parsley sprigs

1 In medium bowl, combine honey, soy sauce, oyster sauce, sugar, ginger, garlic, ketchup, onion powder, cayenne and cinnamon; mix well.

2 Place pork in 13x9-inch pan. Pour honey mixture over pork. Cover; marinate in refrigerator at least 8 hours or up to 24 hours.

3 Grill pork on gas grill over medium heat or on charcoal grill 4 to 6 inches from medium coals. Cook 25 to 30 minutes or until internal temperature reaches 160°F, turning frequently and basting with marinade.* Arrange in thin slices on serving platter. Garnish with parsley.

TIP *To reuse marinade, bring to a boil over high heat before using.

6 servings

CASSOULET WITH LAMB

Lynne Hudson
Chesapeake, Virginia

2 (4- to 6-oz.) lamb shoulder steaks

1 teaspoon herbes de Provence

¼ teaspoon salt

⅛ teaspoon freshly ground pepper

1 tablespoon olive oil

1 medium carrot, finely diced

½ cup chopped yellow onion

2 plum tomatoes, seeded, diced

1 garlic clove, minced

½ cup dry red wine

½ cup veal stock*

1 bay leaf, halved

1 (16-oz.) can white beans, drained

1 Sprinkle lamb with herbes de Provence, salt and pepper. In large skillet, heat oil over medium heat until hot. Add lamb; sauté 5 to 7 minutes or until brown, turning once. Remove from skillet. Cover; set aside.

2 In same large skillet, combine carrot and onion; sauté 2 to 3 minutes. Add tomatoes and garlic; sauté an additional 2 to 3 minutes. Reduce heat to medium-low. Stir in wine, stock and bay leaf; simmer 5 minutes. Add lamb and beans; simmer 15 to 20 minutes or until liquid is reduced. Remove bay leaf.

TIP *Beef stock can be substituted for the veal stock.

2 servings

SOUTH-OF-THE-BORDER CASSEROLE

Elaine Welsh
Rowlett, Texas

1 tablespoon olive oil

1 lb. ground sirloin or ground round

½ cup chopped onions

2 garlic gloves, finely chopped

2 (15½-oz.) cans black-eyed peas, rinsed, drained

1 (10-oz.) can diced tomatoes and green chiles

2 cups cooked long-grain rice

1 teaspoon chili powder

1 teaspoon cumin

¼ teaspoon salt

¼ teaspoon freshly ground pepper

2 cups shredded sharp cheddar cheese (8 oz.)

1 Heat oven to 350°F. Lightly grease 13x9-inch pan. In large skillet, heat oil over medium-high heat until hot. Add beef, onions and garlic; cook until beef is browned and no longer pink in center. Drain excess fat. Add peas, tomatoes, rice, 1 cup cheese, chili powder, cumin, salt and pepper; mix well.

2 Pour into pan. Bake 15 minutes; sprinkle with remaining 1 cup cheese. Bake an additional 5 to 10 minutes.

4 servings

SOUTH-OF-THE-BORDER CASSEROLE

SMOKED SAUSAGE AND NEW POTATOES
WITH BELL PEPPERS AND ONIONS

Greg Bauer
Clinton, Missouri

1 lb. smoked beef or pork sausage, cut in 1/2-inch-thick slices

10 to 12 small new potatoes, quartered

1 medium red bell pepper, cut into match-stick-size pieces

1 medium green bell pepper, cut into match-stick-size pieces

1 small red onion, thinly sliced

1 teaspoon lemon pepper

1/2 teaspoon garlic salt

2 tablespoons butter, cut into small pieces

2 tablespoons chopped fresh parsley

1 Heat oven to 375°F. Spray 3-quart casserole with nonstick cooking spray.

2 Combine sausage, potatoes, red bell pepper, green bell pepper and onion in pan. Sprinkle with pepper and salt; mix well. Top mixture with butter. Bake 1 hour or until very hot and potatoes are tender, stirring once. Sprinkle with parsley.

6 servings

THICK PORK CHOPS ON THE GRILL

Marlene Sinyard
Brunswick, Maine

MARINADE

1/2 cup low-sodium soy sauce

1/2 cup sherry

1 tablespoon sugar

2 garlic cloves, minced

PORK

4 thick-cut bone-in pork chops

1 In blender container, combine soy sauce, sherry, sugar and garlic; blend until smooth.

2 Place pork in resealable plastic bag. Pour marinade over pork; turn pork to coat evenly. Seal bag; refrigerate at least 6 hours or up to 24 hours, turning pork occasionally.

3 Heat grill. Remove pork from marinade; discard marinade. Place pork on gas grill over medium heat or on charcoal grill 4 to 6 inches from medium-low coals. Cook 30 to 40 minutes or until pork is no longer pink in center, turning once.

4 servings

CITRUS-MARINATED PORK TENDERLOIN

Deborah Atkins
Los Banos, California

$\frac{1}{2}$ cup fresh orange juice

$\frac{1}{2}$ cup fresh grapefruit juice

$\frac{1}{2}$ teaspoon salt

$\frac{1}{2}$ teaspoon freshly ground pepper

$\frac{1}{2}$ teaspoon dried thyme

1 tablespoon olive oil

2 lb. pork tenderloins

1 In 3-quart casserole, combine orange juice, grapefruit juice, salt, pepper, thyme and oil; blend well. Add pork; turn to coat all sides. Cover and refrigerate 1 to 3 hours, turning occasionally.

2 Heat grill. Remove pork from marinade; discard marinade. Place pork on gas grill over medium heat or on charcoal grill 4 to 6 inches from medium coals.

3 Cook 20 minutes or until no longer pink in center, turning once. Remove pork from grill. Cover loosely with aluminum foil; let stand 10 minutes before slicing.

6 servings

BEEF CARBONNADE

Tracey Cole
Rowlett, Texas

2 tablespoons vegetable oil

3 lb. beef for stew, cut into cubes

1 large onion, sliced

1 garlic clove, crushed

1 tablespoon all-purpose flour

1 cup brown ale or beer

1 teaspoon vinegar

Salt

Freshly ground pepper

10 slices French bread (1$\frac{1}{2}$-inch)

3 tablespoons Dijon mustard

1 In Dutch oven or large pot, heat oil over medium-high heat until hot. Add beef and onion; cook 7 minutes or until beef is browned. Turn off heat. Using slotted spoon, place beef and onion in crockpot. Add garlic.

2 Stir flour into juices in Dutch oven. Slowly add beer, whisking constantly. Pour over beef; add vinegar. Cook in crockpot on high 4 to 5 hours or until fork tender. Season with salt and pepper.

3 Thirty minutes before serving, spread each bread slice thickly with mustard. Place slices mustard side up on top of beef, pressing down slightly.

4 to 6 servings

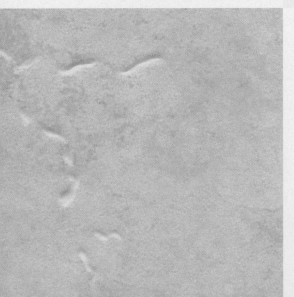

GERMAN-STYLE ROAST

Judi Shadle
Manteo, North Carolina

1 (3½-lb.) chuck roast, trimmed

2 to 3 garlic cloves, sliced

Pinch salt

Pinch freshly ground pepper

2 tablespoons all-purpose flour

3 tablespoons vegetable oil

1 large onion, sliced, separated into rings

1 (5-oz.) jar prepared creamy horseradish

1 (16-oz.) can beer

2 tablespoons cornstarch

4 teaspoons water

1 Heat oven to 350°F. Make slits in roast; fill with garlic. Season with salt and pepper. Roll in enough flour to evenly coat; shake off excess.

2 In Dutch oven or large pot, heat oil over medium-high heat until hot. Add roast; brown on all sides. Add onion, horseradish and beer; bring to a low boil. Remove from heat. Cover; place in oven.

3 Cook 2 to 2½ hours or until roast is fork tender. Remove from oven; place on serving platter.

4 In small bowl, combine cornstarch and water; mix well. Add to mixture in Dutch oven. Bring to a simmer over medium-low heat; simmer 2 to 3 minutes or until thick. Season with additional salt and pepper, if desired. Serve with roast.

4 to 6 servings

PORK WITH GREEN OLIVES AND TOMATOES

Maureen Napier
Cincinnati, Ohio

1 tablespoon olive oil

1 medium onion, chopped

2 garlic cloves, crushed

8 (1-inch-thick) boneless pork chops

1 (16-oz.) can tomato sauce

1 (10-oz.) jar stuffed green olives, drained

1 tablespoon Worcestershire sauce

1 teaspoon garlic powder

¼ teaspoon freshly ground pepper

1 In large skillet, heat oil over medium-high heat until hot. Add onion and garlic; sauté 3 to 5 minutes or until onion is tender.

2 Add pork; cook on both sides until golden brown. Add tomato sauce, olives, Worcestershire sauce, garlic powder and pepper; mix thoroughly. Heat until bubbly. Cover; simmer 15 minutes or until pork is tender.

8 servings

GREAT AUNT KATIE'S SAUSAGE BEROK

Joanna Henry
Houston, Texas

FILLING

$\frac{1}{2}$ lb. lean ground beef

$\frac{1}{2}$ lb. pork sausage

1 head cabbage, chopped

2 medium yellow onions, chopped

DOUGH

$1\frac{1}{4}$ cups warm water (110°F to 115°F)

1 ($\frac{1}{4}$-oz.) pkg. active dry yeast

$\frac{1}{2}$ cup plus 1 tablespoon sugar

2 tablespoons all-purpose flour

1 cup evaporated milk

$\frac{1}{2}$ cup shortening

1 tablespoon salt

1 cup warm mashed potatoes

2 eggs, beaten

$6\frac{1}{2}$ to 7 cups bread flour

6 tablespoons butter, melted

1 Grease baking sheet. Cook beef and pork in Dutch oven or large pot over medium-high heat 5 to 8 minutes or until no longer pink in center. Reduce heat to medium. Add cabbage and onions; cook 1 hour or until mixture is tender and lightly browned. Remove from heat; set aside.

2 In small bowl, combine $\frac{1}{4}$ cup warm water, yeast, 1 tablespoon sugar and flour. Set in warm place until light and bubbly, stirring occasionally.

3 In large saucepan, combine remaining 1 cup water, milk, shortening, salt and remaining $\frac{1}{2}$ cup sugar. Bring to a boil over medium-high heat. Add potatoes; mix well. Remove from heat; cool to room temperature.

4 To potato mixture, add yeast mixture, eggs and enough flour to make smooth dough. Continue to add flour until mixture can be kneaded. Turn out onto lightly floured surface; knead 10 minutes or until smooth and elastic. Place dough in greased bowl. Oil top; cover and let rise 1 hour or until double in size.

5 Divide dough into 4 portions. Roll each portion into a square $\frac{1}{8}$-inch-thick. Cut each portion into 6-inch squares. Place $\frac{1}{4}$ cup cabbage mixture in center of each square. Draw up opposite corners; seal. Place squares, seam side down, on baking sheet. Brush tops with butter. Let rise 15 to 20 minutes.

6 Heat oven to 375°F. Bake 20 to 25 minutes or until lightly browned and cooked through.

30 beroks

BEEF 'N' TATER BAKE

Rose Sienkiewicz
Chandler, Arizona

1 1/2 lb. lean ground beef

1 cup soft bread crumbs

1/2 cup onion, chopped

1 egg, beaten

1/3 cup ketchup

1/2 teaspoon salt

1/4 teaspoon freshly ground pepper

3 cups mashed potatoes

3/4 cup shredded american cheese (4 oz.)

1 Heat oven to 350°F. In large bowl, combine beef, bread crumbs, onion, egg, ketchup, salt and pepper; mix well. Place mixture in 3-quart casserole. Bake 20 minutes. Remove from oven; drain fat.

2 In medium bowl, combine potatoes and 3/4 cup of the cheese; mix well. Spread over beef mixture; top with remaining 1/4 cup cheese. Bake 20 minutes.

6 servings

ANDY'S FAVORITE MEATBALLS

Jennifer Guinea
Minneapolis, Minnesota

1 lb. lean ground beef

1 egg

1/4 cup bread crumbs

3 to 5 garlic cloves, minced

1/2 cup chopped scallions

1/8 teaspoon salt

1/8 teaspoon pepper

1/8 teaspoon garlic powder

1/8 teaspoon onion powder

1 teaspoon Worcestershire sauce

1 teaspoon vegetable oil

1 Heat oven to 350°F. In medium bowl, combine beef, egg, bread crumbs, garlic, scallions, salt, pepper, garlic powder, onion powder, Worcestershire sauce and oil; mix well. Form mixture into 2-inch-thick meatballs. Arrange meatballs on 15x10x1-inch pan. Bake 35 to 40 minutes or until no longer pink in center.

8 meatballs

Poultry

CHICKEN FORMAGGIO PIZZA

CHICKEN FORMAGGIO PIZZA

Sean Pilon
Monroe, Michigan

DOUGH

1 (¼ oz.) pkg. active dry yeast

1 cup warm water (110°F to 115°F)

1 egg

½ teaspoon salt

3½ to 4 cups all-purpose flour

1 tablespoon olive oil

SAUCE

2 (1.25-oz.) pkg. white sauce mix

2¼ cups heavy whipping cream

⅛ teaspoon garlic salt

⅛ teaspoon freshly ground pepper

5 oz. shredded fontina cheese (16 oz.)

TOPPING

½ cup frozen spinach, thawed, squeezed dry

½ cup chopped green onions

1 lb. boneless skinless chicken breast halves, cooked, diced

4 cups shredded mozzarella cheese (16 oz.)

1 In large bowl, dissolve yeast in water. When yeast has softened and become foamy (3 to 4 minutes), stir in egg and salt. Gradually stir in 3½ cups flour; mix until soft dough forms, adding more flour if dough is moist.

2 On lightly floured surface, knead dough 5 minutes or until smooth and elastic. Coat with oil; place in bowl. Cover; let rise 15 minutes. Punch dough to deflate. Divide into 2 sections. Roll each section to fit 14-inch round pizza pan. Cover dough; let rise 20 minutes.

3 In medium saucepan, combine white sauce mix, cream, salt and pepper. Bring to a boil over medium heat. Add fontina cheese; cook until melted, stirring constantly.

4 Heat oven to 375°F. Spread each pizza round with half of cheese sauce. Top each with half of spinach, onions, chicken and mozzarella cheese. Bake 15 to 20 minutes.

2 (14-inch) pizzas

OVEN CHICKEN CACCIATORE

Paula Davis
Athens, Alabama

1 (1-lb.) pkg. vermicelli

6 boneless skinless chicken breast halves

1 medium onion, sliced

1 medium bell pepper, cut into strips

1 medium zucchini, sliced

1 (1-lb.) pkg. sliced fresh mushrooms

1 (4.25-oz.) can sliced ripe olives, drained

1 (28-oz.) can crushed tomatoes

1 (6-oz.) can tomato paste

½ teaspoon salt

½ teaspoon freshly ground pepper

1 teaspoon dried basil

1 teaspoon dried oregano

½ teaspoon garlic powder

Parmesan cheese

1 Cook vermicelli according to package directions.

2 Heat oven to 350°F. Place chicken in 13x9-inch pan. Cover with onion, bell pepper, zucchini, mushrooms and olives.

3 In large bowl, combine tomatoes, tomato paste, salt, pepper, basil, oregano and garlic powder; mix well. Pour over chicken and vegetables. Cover with aluminum foil.

4 Bake 1 hour. Remove foil; bake an additional 30 minutes. Spoon chicken mixture over vermicelli. Sprinkle with cheese.

6 servings

JERK RUB FOR CHICKEN

Carmen Namenek
Anaheim, California

2 bunches green onions, finely chopped

5 to 7 garlic cloves, chopped

1/4 cup chopped ginger

1 1/2 habanero chiles, seeded, stemmed, finely chopped

1/4 cup canola oil

1/2 cup fresh thyme

3 bay leaves

1 tablespoon freshly ground pepper

1 tablespoon ground coriander

1 teaspoon ground cinnamon

2 teaspoons salt

2 teaspoons ground allspice

1 teaspoon ground nutmeg

Juice of 1 lime

1 (3- to 4-lb.) chicken, cut up

1 In blender, combine onions, garlic, ginger, chiles, oil, thyme, bay leaves, pepper, coriander, cinnamon, salt, allspice, nutmeg and lime juice; blend until thick paste forms. *(Rub can be made up to 4 months ahead. Cover and refrigerate.)*

2 Rub 1/2 cup rub on all sides and under skin of chicken pieces. Marinate, covered, in refrigerator 4 hours. (Marinating the chicken longer will increase the spice of the rub.)

3 Heat oven to 375°F. Line 15x10x1-inch baking pan with aluminum foil. Place chicken on pan. Cook 1 hour or until no longer pink in center.

4 to 6 servings

CHICKEN AND CRAB RICHELE

William and Richele Ward
Pittsburgh, Pennsylvania

CHICKEN

10 oz. jumbo lump crabmeat

1 tablespoon finely diced red bell pepper

1 tablespoon finely diced green bell pepper

3 tablespoons mayonnaise

1 tablespoon chopped fresh tarragon

1/8 teaspoon salt

1/8 teaspoon freshly ground pepper

4 (8-oz.) boneless skinless chicken breast halves

SAUCE

2 medium tomatoes, grilled

3 tablespoons olive oil

1 teaspoon minced garlic

1 1/2 teaspoons chopped fresh basil

1/4 teaspoon dried oregano

Pinch salt

1 medium zucchini, cut into 1/4-inch slices

1 Heat oven to 350°F. In medium bowl, combine crabmeat, red bell pepper, green bell pepper, mayonnaise, tarragon, salt and pepper; mix well. Place 1/4 crab mixture in center of each chicken breast; fold over. Place in 13x9-inch pan. Bake 20 to 25 minutes or until chicken is no longer pink in center and internal temperature reaches 160°F.

2 In food processor, combine tomatoes, 2 tablespoons of the oil, garlic, basil, oregano and salt; process until smooth. Pour into small saucepan; heat over low heat to keep warm.

3 In medium skillet, heat oil over medium-high heat until hot. Add zucchini; sauté 3 to 5 minutes or until tender.

4 To serve, place generous 1/4 cup sauce on each plate, covering plate. Place 1 chicken breast in center of each plate. Place zucchini around edges of plates.

4 servings

CHIPOTLE LIME SAUCE

Richard Rands
Woodland Hills, California

- 1 cup sour cream
- 1 canned chipotle chili in adobo sauce, chopped
- 1 tablespoon fresh lime juice
- 1 tablespoon minced fresh cilantro
- ¼ teaspoon salt
- ¼ teaspoon freshly ground pepper

In food processor, combine sour cream, chili, lime juice, cilantro, salt and pepper; process 1 minute or until well mixed. Serve with grilled fish or poultry, or as a dip for vegetables or tortilla chips.

1½ cups

MESSY CHICKEN

Myrna Zelin
Brooklyn, New York

- 2 lb. chicken legs
- 2 lb. chicken wings (tips removed)
- Dash salt
- Dash freshly ground pepper
- ¾ cup honey
- ⅓ cup low-sodium soy sauce
- 3 tablespoons ketchup
- 2 tablespoons vegetable oil
- 2 large garlic cloves, minced

1 Heat oven to 350°F. Spray 13x9-inch pan with nonstick cooking spray. Season chicken with salt and pepper; place in pan.

2 In medium bowl, combine honey, soy sauce, ketchup, oil and garlic; mix well. Pour over chicken. Bake 45 minutes; turn chicken. Bake an additional 20 minutes or until chicken is no longer pink in center.

6 to 8 servings

CHICKEN ADOBO

Leslie Burke
Captain Cook, Hawaii

CHICKEN

- 4 lb. chicken thighs, skin on
- 2 to 3 tablespoons peanut oil

MARINADE

- 1 cup chicken stock
- ½ cup rice vinegar
- ¼ cup red wine vinegar
- ¼ cup low-sodium soy sauce
- 4 garlic cloves, chopped
- 2 to 3 bay leaves
- 1 tablespoon freshly grated ginger
- 1 teaspoon paprika
- ½ teaspoon freshly ground pepper
- Salt

1 Cut chicken thighs into 12 pieces; trim fat. In small bowl, combine broth, rice vinegar, red wine vinegar, soy sauce, garlic, bay leaves, ginger, paprika, pepper and salt; mix well. Pour into 13x9-inch pan. Add chicken. Cover; marinate in refrigerator at least 30 minutes or up to 2 hours. Remove chicken from marinade; pat dry. Reserve marinade.

2 In nonreactive Dutch oven or large skillet, heat oil over medium-high heat until hot. Add chicken; brown on all sides. Pour reserved marinade over chicken; bring to a boil. Reduce heat to low. Cover; simmer 20 to 30 minutes or until chicken is no longer pink in center. Skim fat from marinade; season with additional salt and pepper, if desired. Serve with chicken.

6 to 8 servings

CHICKEN BOG

Julie Nyberg
Fort Wayne, Indiana

1 (4-lb.) chicken, cut up

$\frac{1}{4}$ teaspoon plus pinch salt

$\frac{1}{8}$ teaspoon plus pinch freshly ground pepper

2 chicken bouillon cubes

1 lb. smoked sausage, cut into $\frac{1}{2}$-inch coins

2 cups rice

1 Season chicken with pinch each of the salt and pepper. In Dutch oven or large pot, combine chicken, bouillon cubes and enough water to cover chicken. Bring mixture just to a boil over medium heat; reduce heat to low. Cook, covered, 1 hour or until chicken is well done. Remove from broth, reserving 5 cups broth. Cool chicken; debone.

2 In large saucepan, combine reserved broth, chicken pieces, sausage, $\frac{1}{4}$ teaspoon salt and $\frac{1}{8}$ teaspoon pepper. Bring to a boil over medium-high heat; add rice. Reduce heat to low. Cook, covered, 20 to 25 minutes or until most liquid is absorbed and rice is fully cooked, stirring occasionally.

6 ($1\frac{3}{4}$-cup) servings

SUNDAY CHICKEN WITH SAUSAGE AND POLENTA

Jean McCormick
Deer Park, New York

CHICKEN

3 tablespoons olive oil

1 ($3\frac{1}{2}$- to 4-lb.) chicken, cut up

$1\frac{1}{2}$ lb. sweet or hot Italian sausage links, cut into 3-inch pieces

3 large Spanish onions, cut into $\frac{1}{2}$-inch rings, halved

2 to 3 sprigs fresh rosemary or 1 tablespoon dried

1 (28-oz.) can tomato puree

$\frac{1}{2}$ teaspoon salt

$\frac{1}{2}$ teaspoon freshly ground pepper

POLENTA

1 cup coarse yellow cornmeal

3 cups cold water

2 teaspoons salt

1 In large skillet, heat oil over medium-high heat until hot. Add chicken; cook 5 minutes or until browned. Remove from skillet. Add sausage to same large skillet; cook 2 to 3 minutes or until browned. Remove; drain on paper towels.

2 In same skillet, add onions; sauté 3 to 5 minutes or until transparent. Add rosemary, chicken and tomato puree; mix well. Stir in $\frac{1}{2}$ teaspoon salt and pepper. Reduce heat to low; cover. Cook 1 hour.

3 To make polenta, in medium saucepan, combine cornmeal and water; mix well. Stir in 2 teaspoons salt. Bring to a boil over medium-high heat. Reduce heat to low; simmer 20 minutes or until mixture pulls away from side of saucepan, stirring often. Pour mixture onto large wooden board or flat baking sheet; let stand 5 minutes. Using unwaxed dental floss, cut into 6 or 8 wedges.

4 To serve, place 1 wedge polenta on each plate. Top with chicken, sausage and sauce.

6 to 8 servings

SUNDAY CHICKEN WITH SAUSAGE AND POLENTA

CHICKEN PICCATA

CHICKEN PICCATA

Wallace Light
Sunnyvale, California

2 tablespoons vegetable oil

4 green onions, chopped

2 garlic cloves, minced

1 small onion, chopped

½ cup all-purpose flour

Salt

Freshly ground pepper

8 boneless skinless chicken breast halves, pounded flat

2 tablespoons butter

2 tablespoons dry sherry

2 tablespoons fresh lemon juice

1 tablespoon chopped capers

¾ cup chicken stock

8 thin slices lemon

2 tablespoons chopped fresh parsley

1 In large skillet, heat oil over medium-high heat until hot. Add green onions, garlic and onion; sauté 3 to 4 minutes or just until onion is tender. Remove from pan; set aside.

2 In small bowl, combine flour, salt and pepper; dredge chicken breasts in flour mixture, patting off excess. In same skillet, melt butter over medium-high heat. Add chicken; cook 4 to 6 minutes or until lightly brown and no longer pink in center, turning once. Remove from pan; cover loosely with aluminum foil.

3 Add sautéed onions and garlic to skillet. Add sherry, lemon juice, capers and stock; cook over high heat 5 to 10 minutes or until sauce thickens. If sauce becomes too thick, thin with additional chicken stock.

4 Serve chicken with sauce. Garnish with lemon and parsley.

8 servings

TURKEY BUNDLES WITH SPINACH

Melody Brown
Brooklyn, New York

⅔ cup frozen chopped spinach, thawed, drained

½ cup part-skim ricotta cheese

¼ cup freshly grated Parmesan cheese (1 oz.)

2 egg whites

8 (4-oz.) turkey cutlets, pounded ¼ inch thick

½ teaspoon plus dash salt

1 teaspoon freshly ground pepper

¼ cup all-purpose flour

4 teaspoons olive oil

2 (14½-oz.) cans stewed chopped tomatoes

¼ cup chopped fresh parsley

2 tablespoons tomato paste

1 In small bowl, combine spinach, ricotta cheese, Parmesan cheese and egg whites; mix well.

2 Sprinkle each turkey cutlet with dash salt and pepper; spread each with spinach mixture. Roll up cutlets tightly, starting with short end. Secure rolls with toothpick.

3 Sprinkle flour on parchment paper; dredge cutlets in flour, patting off excess.

4 In large skillet, heat oil over medium heat until hot. Add cutlets seam side down; cook 4 minutes or until browned, turning frequently. Add tomatoes, parsley, tomato paste and ½ teaspoon salt. Reduce heat to medium; simmer, covered, 10 minutes or until turkey is no longer pink in center.

5 To serve, spoon sauce onto large serving platter or individual plates. Place cutlets on top of sauce.

4 servings

ROSEMARY CHICKEN IN ARTICHOKE SAUCE

Marguerite Chaikin-Johnstone
Austin, Texas

MARINADE

3 garlic cloves, minced

1 tablespoon Dijon mustard

1/4 cup olive oil

1/4 cup cider vinegar

2 teaspoons minced fresh rosemary

CHICKEN

4 (6-oz.) boneless skinless chicken breast halves

SAUCE

2 tablespoons butter

1 small leek (white part only), halved lengthwise, sliced

1 (12 oz.) jar marinated artichoke hearts, drained, liquid reserved

1/2 cup chicken stock

1 1/2 cup heavy whipping cream

1 In resealable plastic bag, combine garlic, mustard, oil, vinegar and rosemary; mix well. Place chicken in marinade; turn to coat evenly. Seal bag; refrigerate at least 4 hours or up to 6 hours, turning chicken occasionally.

2 Melt 1 tablespoon of the butter in large skillet over medium heat. Remove chicken from marinade; discard marinade. Place chicken in skillet; sauté 10 to 14 minutes or until no longer pink in center, turning once. Remove from skillet; cover loosely with aluminum foil.

3 Melt remaining 1 tablespoon butter in same large skillet. Add leek; sauté 1 minute or until barely tender. Add reserved artichoke liquid and stock. Simmer 5 to 7 minutes or until reduced by half. Add artichoke hearts and cream; simmer 5 to 7 minutes or until sauce is reduced and slightly thickened, stirring frequently.

4 Pour sauce over serving platter; top with chicken.

4 servings

CHICKEN FIESTA

Mae Felder
Houston, Texas

2 tablespoons butter

2 lb. boneless skinless chicken breast halves, cut into 1-inch cubes

1 1/2 lb. mushrooms, sliced

1 cup chicken stock

1 1/2 cups picante sauce

1 tablespoon garlic powder

1/2 teaspoon salt

1/2 teaspoon freshly ground pepper

1 teaspoon dried oregano

1 cup grated Monterey Jack and colby cheeses (4 oz.)

1 In nonreactive Dutch oven or large pot, melt butter over medium-high heat. Add chicken; cook 10 minutes. Add mushrooms; cook 5 minutes. Drain excess liquid.

2 Stir in broth, picante sauce, garlic powder, salt, pepper and oregano; simmer 15 to 20 minutes. Serve over rice, noodles or baked potatoes, if desired. Top with cheese.

6 to 8 servings

MUSTARD BASTING SAUCE FOR CHICKEN

Rosemary Siewert
Apple Valley, Minnesota

1/2 cup butter

1/3 cup chopped shallots

3 tablespoons Dijon mustard

1 tablespoon grated lemon peel

2 tablespoons olive oil

2 tablespoons fresh lemon juice

In small saucepan, melt butter over medium heat. Remove from heat; add shallots, mustard, lemon peel, oil and lemon juice. Whisk until mixture is smooth. Use to baste chicken or fresh vegetables.

1 1/4 cups

Fish & Seafood

SPINACH FETTUCCINE WITH SCALLOPS

Priscilla Migliore
Sherman Oaks, California

1 (1-lb.) pkg. spinach fettuccine

2 tablespoons olive oil

12 to 16 oz. bay scallops

1/4 cup chopped yellow onion

1 garlic clove, minced

1/2 cup heavy cream

3/4 teaspoon salt

1/4 teaspoon ground white pepper

2 medium plum tomatoes, diced

Freshly grated Parmesan cheese

1 Cook fettuccine according to package directions.

2 In large skillet, heat oil over medium-high heat until hot. Add scallops, onion and garlic; sauté 5 minutes or until scallops are almost cooked through. Add fettuccine and cream; cook 3 minutes. Remove from heat. Season with salt and pepper. Garnish with tomatoes and cheese.

4 to 6 servings

SEAFOOD GUMBO

Richard Rands
Woodland Hills, California

1/2 cup vegetable oil

3/4 cup all-purpose flour

1 medium tomato, chopped

1 cup finely chopped onion

1/2 cup finely chopped celery

1/2 cup finely chopped green bell pepper

1 1/2 teaspoons minced garlic

1 1/2 teaspoons Cajun seasoning

4 oz. andouille or smoked sausage

1 1/2 quarts chicken stock

1/2 lb. shelled, deveined uncooked medium shrimp

1/2 lb. crabmeat

1 cup oysters with liquid

1/4 cup chopped green onions with tops

1/4 cup minced parsley

1 1/2 teaspoons filé powder

2 cups cooked rice

1 In large skillet, heat oil over medium-high heat until hot. Reduce heat to medium-low. Add flour; whisk until mixture is rich golden brown.

2 Add tomato, onion, celery, bell pepper, garlic and Cajun seasoning to skillet; cook 5 minutes. Add sausage; cook an additional 5 minutes. Slowly add all stock except 1/2 cup; stir until well combined. Simmer 30 minutes. Add shrimp, crabmeat, oysters, green onions and parsley; simmer 5 minutes. Remove from heat.

3 In small bowl, combine filé powder and remaining 1/2 cup stock. Stir into shrimp mixture.

4 To serve, place 1/2 cup rice in center of individual serving bowl; ladle seafood mixture over rice. Repeat with remaining rice and shrimp mixture.

4 servings

SHRIMP SICILIAN

Tony Calabria
Chicago, Illinois

2 tablespoons olive oil

1 tablespoon minced garlic

¾ lb. shelled, deveined uncooked large shrimp

1½ teaspoons chopped fresh oregano

1½ teaspoons chopped fresh basil

8 cherry tomatoes, halved

¼ cup Spanish green olives

¼ cup drained pitted ripe olives

8 cherry peppers, halved, seeded

8 pepperoncini peppers, stemmed, halved, seeded

¼ cup seasoned dry bread crumbs

1 In large skillet or wok, heat oil over medium-high heat until hot. Add garlic; cook until lightly browned. Add shrimp, oregano and basil; cook 2 minutes.

2 Add cherry tomatoes; cook an additional 2 minutes. Add green olives, ripe olives, cherry peppers and pepperoncini peppers; cook just until shrimp turn pink and are firm.

3 Add bread crumbs; toss until shrimp and peppers are thoroughly coated and all liquid is absorbed. Serve immediately.

2 servings

POACHED SCALLOPS WITH CURRY

William Wortman Jr.
Cornelious, North Carolina

1 tablespoon butter

1 leek (white part only), cut into matchstick-size pieces

1 carrot, cut into matchstick-size pieces

1 rib celery, diced

½ medium onion, diced

2 teaspoons curry powder

1 cup white wine

1 cup water

8 large sea scallops

Salt

Freshly ground white pepper

1 In large skillet, melt butter over medium-high heat. Add leek, carrot, celery and onion; sauté 4 to 5 minutes or until vegetables are just tender. Add curry powder; stir to coat. Add wine and water; bring to a boil. Reduce heat to medium; simmer until liquid is slightly reduced and vegetables are soft.

2 Cut each scallop horizontally into 3 pieces. Cook in curry mixture 2 to 3 minutes or until scallops are opaque. Season with salt and pepper.

3 To serve, place scallops in bowl. Strain wine mixture over top. Top with fennel or chervil, if desired. Serve vegetables on side.

2 servings

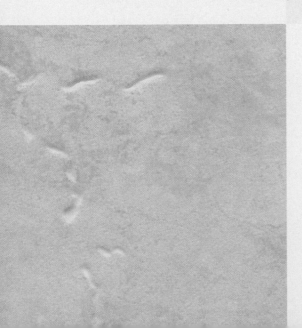

SHRIMP WITH TASSO GRAVY

Richard Rands
Woodland Hills, California

2 tablespoons olive oil

2 tablespoons chopped mild Italian sausage

2 tablespoons minced tasso ham*

1 garlic clove, minced

2 tablespoons chopped green onions

2 tablespoons bread flour

1 cup chicken stock

8 oz. shelled, deveined uncooked medium shrimp

2 cups cooked rice

1 tablespoon sliced green onion tops

1 In large skillet, heat oil over medium-high heat until hot. Add sausage and ham; sauté until light brown. Add garlic and green onions; sauté 2 minutes. Stir in flour; cook 2 minutes. Slowly whisk in stock; cook until mixture thickens. Cover; reduce heat to low.

2 In another large skillet heat remaining 1 tablespoon oil over medium-high heat until hot. Add shrimp; sauté until shrimp turn pink.

3 Place rice on serving platter; pour ham sauce over rice. Top with shrimp. Garnish with onion tops.

TIP *Regular ham can be substituted, but it will affect the taste.

2 servings

SPICY SHRIMP WILLIAM

William and Richele Ward
Pittsburgh, Pennsylvania

1 tablespoon olive oil

1 tablespoon butter

1 tablespoon minced celery

1 tablespoon minced onion

1 garlic clove, minced

$\frac{1}{8}$ teaspoon crushed red pepper

$\frac{1}{2}$ cup diced tomatoes

$\frac{1}{4}$ cup diced red bell pepper

16 shelled, deveined uncooked medium shrimp (about $\frac{1}{2}$ lb.)

2 tablespoons white wine

1 tablespoon fresh lemon juice

Salt

Freshly ground pepper

2 sprigs fresh parsley

1 teaspoon chopped fresh cilantro

2 cups cooked rice

1 In large skillet, heat oil and butter over medium-high heat until butter is melted. Add celery, onion, garlic, red pepper flakes, tomatoes and bell pepper; sauté 8 minutes or until vegetables are very tender. Add shrimp, wine and lemon juice; sauté 5 minutes or until shrimp turn pink. Sprinkle with salt, pepper, parsley and cilantro.

2 Place 1 cup rice in center of each plate. Add sauce around rice; place 8 shrimp around edge of each plate.

2 servings

SPICY SHRIMP WILLIAM

MUSSELS IN SAFFRON BROTH

Richard Rands
Woodland Hills, California

1 tablespoon butter

1 tablespoon finely chopped green onions

1 cup chicken stock

1 cup white wine

2 lb. mussels, cleaned

¼ cup heavy cream

Pinch saffron

Pinch ground white pepper

1 tablespoon minced fresh parsley

1 In nonreactive Dutch oven or large pot, melt butter over medium-high heat. Add onions, broth and wine; bring to a boil. Add mussels. Cover; cook 5 minutes or until all mussels have opened.* Remove mussels; divide into 2 large shallow bowls.

2 Add cream, saffron and pepper to broth. Bring to a boil; cook 5 minutes. Add parsley; ladle sauce over mussels.

TIP * Mussels that do not open during cooking are inedible and should be discarded.

2 servings

TUNA FIORINTINO

Nancy Bruno
Valley Cottage, New York

1 (16-oz.) pkg. linguine or spaghetti

1 to 2 tablespoons olive oil

1 small onion, chopped

4 garlic cloves, minced

1 (28-oz.) can crushed tomatoes

1 teaspoon dried basil

1 teaspoon dried oregano

Salt

Freshly ground pepper

Crushed red pepper

1½ cups dry white wine

1 (8-oz.) tuna steak

1 Cook linguine according to package directions.

2 In large skillet, heat oil over medium-high heat until hot. Add onion; sauté 5 to 6 minutes or until golden. Add garlic; cook 1 to 2 minutes or until garlic is slightly yellow. Stir in tomatoes. Add basil, oregano, salt, pepper and red pepper flakes; cook until warm. Add 1 cup wine; bring mixture to a simmer. Add tuna; cover with sauce.

3 Reduce heat to medium-low; cover. Cook 30 minutes. Reduce heat to low; stir in remaining ½ cup wine. Cook 1 hour, stirring occasionally.

4 Before serving, flake tuna into sauce in small shreds. Serve over linguine.

4 servings

MUSSELS IN WHITE WINE

Marlene Sinyard
Brunswick, Maine

5 tablespoons olive oil

8 garlic cloves, chopped

1 cup chopped shallots

1 cup chopped onion

1 teaspoon chili powder

1 teaspoon oregano

4 lb. mussels

1 cup white wine

¼ cup butter

Juice from 2 lemons

2 tablespoons chopped fresh parsley

1 In nonreactive Dutch oven or large pot, heat oil over medium-high heat until hot. Add garlic; sauté 1 to 2 minutes or until golden. Add shallots, onion, chili powder and oregano; sauté 4 to 5 minutes or until onion is transparent. Stir in mussels, wine, butter and lemon juice.

2 Raise heat to medium-high. Steam mussels 5 minutes. Discard any unopened mussels.* Garnish with parsley.

TIP * Mussels that do not open during cooking are inedible and should be discarded.

4 servings

PIZZA RUSTICA

Maria DiFalco
Arvada, Colorado

DOUGH

¾ cup margarine, softened

3 cups all-purpose flour

2 eggs, slightly beaten

1 to 2 tablespoons water

1 egg yolk, slightly beaten

FILLING

1¼ cups ricotta cheese

½ lb. mozzarella cheese, diced

⅓ lb. provolone cheese, diced

1⅓ cups freshly grated Parmesan cheese

4 eggs, slightly beaten

½ lb. smoked hard salmon, diced

3 medium garlic cloves, minced

¼ cup chopped fresh parsley

1 Heat oven to 375°F. In large bowl, cut margarine into flour with pastry blender. Add 2 eggs and water; mix until dough holds together. Cover with damp cloth; refrigerate 30 minutes.

2 In another large bowl, combine all cheeses, eggs, salmon, garlic and parsley; mix well.

3 Divide dough into 2 portions. Roll 1 portion between parchment paper to fit sides and bottom of 11x9x2-inch pan. Spoon filling over dough, spreading evenly. Roll out remaining dough between waxed paper to fit top. Moisten dough edges with water or milk; pinch together to seal. Prick top layer of dough with fork; brush with egg yolk.

4 Bake 45 to 60 minutes or until knife inserted near center comes out clean. Cool on wire rack 20 minutes before serving.

6 servings

ASPARAGUS AND SHRIMP PENNE WITH SAFFRON

ASPARAGUS AND SHRIMP PENNE WITH SAFFRON

William Wortman Jr.
Cornelious, North Carolina

1 (1-lb.) pkg. penne

1 cup white wine

¼ teaspoon lightly packed saffron

2 lb. asparagus, cut diagonally into 1-inch pieces

2 tablespoons olive oil

1 lb. shelled, deveined uncooked medium shrimp

¼ cup minced shallots or onions

1¼ cups chicken stock

1 cup heavy whipping cream

Salt

Freshly ground pepper

¼ cup chopped fresh chives

1 Cook penne according to package directions.

2 In small bowl, combine wine and saffron; steep 20 to 30 minutes.

3 In large saucepan, boil 2 to 3 cups salted water. Add asparagus; cook 2 to 3 minutes or just until tender. Drain.

4 In same saucepan, heat oil over medium-high heat until hot. Add shrimp; sauté 4 to 5 minutes or until shrimp turn pink. Set aside.

5 Add shallots and saffron-wine mixture to saucepan; boil until almost all liquid evaporates, making sure mixture does not burn. Add broth and cream; simmer until reduced by half, stirring occasionally. Add asparagus and shrimp; simmer about 2 minutes or until thoroughly heated.

6 In large bowl, combine penne and shrimp mixture. Season with salt and pepper. Garnish with chives.

6 servings

CAJUN BARBECUE SHRIMP

Richard Rands
Woodland Hills, California

½ cup butter

1 teaspoon minced garlic

½ teaspoon ground red pepper

½ teaspoon freshly ground pepper

½ teaspoon dried thyme

½ teaspoon dried oregano

½ teaspoon dried basil

½ teaspoon dried rosemary

½ teaspoon salt

1 tablespoon Worcestershire sauce

½ teaspoon fresh lemon juice

4 oz. beer

12 shelled, deveined uncooked jumbo shrimp

In large saucepan, combine butter, garlic, red pepper, black pepper, thyme, oregano, basil, rosemary, salt, Worcestershire sauce, lemon juice and beer; bring to a boil over medium-high heat. Add shrimp; stir to coat with sauce. Reduce heat to medium; simmer 5 to 7 minutes or until shrimp turn pink.

2 servings

BAKED SALMON CAKES

Bonnie Bowers
Volcano, California

CAKES

1 (14³⁄4-oz.) can salmon, drained, skin and bones removed

¹⁄2 cup mashed potatoes*

1 egg, beaten

¹⁄2 cup reduced-fat sour cream

¹⁄4 cup thinly sliced green onions

¹⁄2 teaspoon salt

¹⁄4 teaspoon freshly ground pepper

¹⁄4 teaspoon paprika

1 tablespoon minced shallots

¹⁄4 teaspoon dry mustard

2 tablespoons chopped fresh parsley

1 teaspoon Worcestershire sauce

2 cups fresh bread crumbs

2 tablespoons butter, melted

LEMON SAUCE

2 tablespoons butter

2 tablespoons all-purpose flour

1 cup milk

2 tablespoons fresh lemon juice

¹⁄4 teaspoon salt

¹⁄8 teaspoon ground red pepper

1 Heat oven to 350°F. Grease baking sheet. In medium bowl, combine salmon, potatoes, egg, sour cream, onions, shallots, ¹⁄2 teaspoon salt, black pepper, paprika, mustard, parsley, Worcestershire sauce and ¹⁄2 cup bread crumbs.

2 Divide mixture into 8 equal portions. Shape each portion into 4-inch patty. Dip each patty in remaining 1¹⁄2 cups bread crumbs; press bread crumbs into patties. Place on baking sheet; drizzle with 2 tablespoons melted butter. Bake 45 minutes or until light brown.

3 To make lemon sauce, melt 2 tablespoons butter in small saucepan over medium heat. Stir in flour until smooth paste forms. Gradually stir in milk; bring to a boil, stirring constantly. Cook 2 minutes or until thickened. Remove from heat; stir in lemon juice, ¹⁄4 teaspoon salt and red pepper.

4 Serve cakes with lemon sauce.

TIP *An additional ¹⁄2 cup unseasoned bread crumbs can be substituted for the mashed potatoes.

4 servings

SHRIMP SCAMPI

Priscilla Migliore
Sherman Oaks, California

1 lb. cleaned, deveined jumbo shrimp butterflied

2 tablespoons butter, melted

2 large garlic cloves, minced

Juice from 1 large lemon

1 teaspoon seasoned salt

Freshly ground pepper

¼ cup chopped fresh parsley or cilantro

1 (1-lb.) pkg. thin linguine

1 Heat oven to 400°F. In 2-quart casserole, combine shrimp, butter, garlic, lemon juice, salt, pepper and parsley; mix well. Bake 15 to 20 minutes or until shrimp turn pink.

2 Meanwhile, cook linguine according to package directions. Toss with shrimp mixture. Sprinkle with freshly grated Parmesan cheese, if desired.

4 to 5 servings

HONEY-LIME MARINATED SWORDFISH

Greta Jones
Palm Harbor, Florida

2 teaspoons grated lime peel

¼ cup fresh lime juice

2 tablespoons honey

2 tablespoons olive oil

⅓ cup coarsely chopped fresh cilantro

1½ lb. swordfish steaks

1 In 3-quart casserole, combine lime peel, juice, honey and oil; mix well. Stir in cilantro. Add swordfish, turning to coat evenly. Cover; refrigerate 30 minutes, turning swordfish occasionally.

2 Heat broiler. Lightly spray broiler pan with nonstick cooking spray. Place swordfish on broiler pan; discard marinade. Broil 4 to 6 inches from heat 8 to 10 minutes or until fish just begins to flake.

4 servings

DISTANT AND DELICIOUS BROILED SALMON

Annette Baran
Santa Monica, California

½ cup sake

½ cup mirin wine*

2 tablespoons low-sodium soy sauce

1 teaspoon minced fresh garlic

1 teaspoon minced fresh ginger

1 (3-lb.) salmon fillet

Chopped fresh parsley

Freshly grated lemon peel

1 In small bowl, combine sake, wine, soy sauce, garlic and ginger; mix well. Pour into 3-quart casserole. Add salmon skin side up. Cover; refrigerate 2 to 4 hours.

2 Place oven rack on lowest position in oven. Heat broiler. Leave ¼-inch marinade in pan; reserve remaining marinade. Broil salmon, skin side up, 20 minutes or until skin chars and puffs up. Remove from oven. Discard marinade in pan. Remove skin from fish; discard skin. Trim salmon of any fat and remaining bones. Sprinkle with parsley and lemon peel.

3 In small saucepan, cook reserved marinade over medium-high heat until reduced by half; strain. Season with salt and pepper. Serve with salmon.

TIP *Mirin wine is available in Asian markets.

8 servings

LOBSTER PASTA RICHELE

William and Richele Ward
Pittsburgh, Pennsylvania

1 lb. farfalle (bow-tie pasta)

2 tablespoons butter

1 garlic clove, minced

2 tablespoons diced onion

1 lb. lobster

4 oz. mushrooms, sliced

2 oz. spinach, rinsed, drained (about 2 cups, tightly packed)

1/4 cup diced tomato

1 small head broccoli florets, blanched

1 tablespoon finely chopped fresh basil

1/2 teaspoon dried oregano

Salt

Freshly ground pepper

2 tablespoons freshly grated Parmesan cheese

1 Cook farfalle according to package directions.

2 In large skillet, melt butter over medium-high heat. Add garlic and onion; sauté 1 minute. Add lobster and mushrooms; cook 7 to 10 minutes or until lobster is firm. Add spinach, tomato, broccoli, basil and oregano; cook 5 minutes. Sprinkle with salt and pepper.

3 Arrange vegetables over farfalle; top with lobster. Sprinkle with cheese.

4 1/3 cups

SANTA FE SEAFOOD STEW

Kimberly Antal
Longmeadow, Massachusetts

1/4 cup olive oil

2 medium zucchini, coarsely chopped

2 medium onions, coarsely chopped

1 large red bell pepper, diced

1 large yellow bell pepper, diced

4 to 5 garlic cloves, minced

2 (28-oz.) cans diced tomatoes

8 oz. mushrooms, thickly sliced

1/2 cup chopped fresh cilantro

2 tablespoons chili powder

1 tablespoon cumin

1 tablespoon dried basil

1 tablespoon dried oregano

2 teaspoons freshly ground pepper

1 teaspoon fennel seeds

1 cup cooked kidney beans

1 cup cooked garbanzo beans

1 lb. shelled, deveined uncooked medium shrimp

1/2 lb. crabmeat

2 tablespoons fresh lemon juice

1 In large skillet, heat oil over medium-high heat until hot. Add zucchini; sauté 6 to 8 minutes or until tender. Remove zucchini; place in large saucepan.

2 In same skillet, sauté onions, red bell pepper, yellow bell pepper and garlic 8 to 10 minutes or until vegetables are tender. Remove vegetables; add to large saucepan containing zucchini.

3 Heat zucchini mixture over low heat. Add tomatoes with juice, mushrooms, cilantro, chili powder, cumin, basil, oregano, pepper and fennel; cook, uncovered, 30 minutes, stirring often. Stir in kidney beans and garbanzo beans; cook an additional 10 minutes. Add shrimp and crabmeat; cook 5 minutes or until shrimp turn pink. Stir in lemon juice.

4 Serve stew over rice or couscous. Garnish with lemon slices and cilantro, or sprinkle with shredded Monterey Jack cheese, if desired.

6 to 8 servings

SANTA FE SEAFOOD STEW

ITALIAN SHRIMP FETTUCCINE

Ellen Ziarko
Grayslake, Illinois

2 tablespoons olive oil

1 cup sliced mushrooms

4 green onions, sliced

1 tablespoon minced garlic

2 (14.5-oz.) cans diced tomatoes

½ cup chopped fresh parsley

¼ cup white wine

1 (8-oz.) pkg. fettuccine

½ lb. shelled, deveined uncooked medium shrimp

2 tablespoons fresh lemon juice

1 In large skillet, heat oil over medium heat until hot. Add mushrooms, green onions and garlic; sauté 1 to 2 minutes. Stir in tomatoes, parsley and wine. Bring to a boil. Reduce heat; simmer 18 to 20 minutes to allow flavors to blend.

2 Meanwhile, cook fettuccine according to package directions.

3 Add shrimp and lemon juice to tomato mixture; cook 1 to 2 minutes or until shrimp turn pink. Serve over fettuccine.

4 servings

JAMAICAN SHRIMP CURRY

Ingrid Falloon
Duluth, Georgia

3 tablespoons butter

1 cup chopped onions

1 garlic clove, minced

3 tablespoons curry powder

2 lb. shelled, deveined uncooked medium shrimp

¼ cup water

2 teaspoons seasoned salt

1 to 2 teaspoons pepper

1 medium cabbage, sliced

6 cups hot cooked rice

1 In large skillet, melt butter over medium heat. Add onion, garlic and curry powder; cook about 5 minutes, stirring frequently, until onion is tender.

2 Stir in shrimp, water, salt and pepper. Add cabbage; cook 10 to 15 minutes or until cabbage is crisp-tender, stirring occasionally. Serve over rice.

6 servings

Meatless

PEPPER AND POTATO OMELET

Richard Rands
Woodland Hills, California

1 teaspoon olive oil

1 teaspoon butter

1/2 medium potato, cut into 1/4-inch cubes

1/4 cup chopped red onion

1/4 cup sliced mushrooms (about 3 medium)

1 tablespoon minced red bell pepper

1 tablespoon minced yellow bell pepper

1 tablespoon minced green bell pepper

1 1/2 teaspoons minced jalapeño chile

1 tablespoon minced fresh parsley

Salt

Freshly ground white pepper

4 eggs

1 In medium skillet, heat oil and butter over medium heat. When butter is melted, add potato; sauté 4 to 5 minutes or until brown. Add red onion, mushrooms, bell peppers, chile, parsley, salt and pepper; sauté 4 to 5 minutes.

2 In small bowl, whisk eggs until blended. Heat small skillet over medium heat until hot. Pour half of whisked eggs into skillet; cook 2 to 3 minutes. Lift edges of egg mixture with fork to allow uncooked mixture to run to bottom. When eggs are set, remove from heat and cover 2 minutes to finish cooking. Slide onto serving plate. Repeat with remaining eggs. Fill each omelet with half of vegetable mixture.

2 omelets

JAVANESE PEANUT PASTA

Kimberly Antal
Longmeadow, Massachusetts

2 tablespoons peanut oil

1 teaspoon crushed red pepper

4 green onions, trimmed, chopped

2 tablespoons packed brown sugar

1/4 cup rice wine vinegar

3 tablespoons low-sodium soy sauce

1 teaspoon sesame oil

1 garlic clove, minced

1 teaspoon freshly grated ginger

1 cup chunky peanut butter

1 cup chicken stock

1 lb. fettuccine

GARNISH

1/2 cup chopped toasted peanuts

2 green onions, sliced

1 medium cucumber, halved, seeded, thinly sliced

1 red bell pepper, cut into thin strips

1/4 cup shredded coconut, if desired

1 In medium skillet, heat oil over low heat until hot. Add red pepper; cook 1 minute. Increase heat to medium. Add chopped green onions; sauté briefly. Remove from heat. Stir in brown sugar, vinegar, soy sauce, sesame oil, garlic and ginger; mix thoroughly. Return skillet to low heat. Add peanut butter 1/4 cup at a time, stirring constantly. Add broth, stirring constantly. Heat until very hot.

2 Place fettuccine in large bowl. Add peanut butter mixture; toss to combine. Sprinkle with peanuts and sliced green onions. Place cucumber slices in concentric circles around pasta. Arrange red pepper strips to radiate from center. Sprinkle pasta with coconut.

4 to 6 servings

RALPH'S WAFFLES

Margo Steinmetz
Cayucos, California

2 cups all-purpose flour

4 teaspoons baking powder

1 tablespoon sugar

1 teaspoon salt

2 cups milk

3 eggs, separated

4 tablespoons butter, melted

1 In large bowl, combine flour, baking powder, sugar, salt, milk and egg yolks; beat until well combined.

2 In medium bowl, beat egg whites until stiff peaks form. Fold into flour mixture. Gently fold in butter.

3 Grease waffle iron. For each waffle, pour ¼ cup batter onto iron. Cook 1 to 2 minutes.

20 waffles

CREAMY SCRAMBLED EGGS

Mable Watson
Lenoi, North Carolina

8 eggs

2 tablespoons water

1 tablespoon butter

1 (3-oz.) pkg. cream cheese (softened), cut into ½-inch cubes

2 tablespoons chopped fresh chives

Salt

Freshly ground pepper

1 In medium bowl, whisk together eggs and water.

2 In large skillet, melt butter over medium heat. Add eggs; cook 3 to 5 minutes or until half cooked. Stir in cream cheese and chives; cook an additional 1 to 2 minutes or until eggs are done. Season with salt and pepper.

4 servings

TOFU AND BROCCOLI PIE

Patricia Bruce
New York, New York

1 small onion, chopped

½ red bell pepper, chopped

3 garlic cloves, finely chopped

1 lb. firm tofu

1 teaspoon dry mustard

1 teaspoon fresh lemon juice

⅛ teaspoon salt

⅓ cup freshly grated Parmesan cheese

1 egg yolk

1 cup frozen chopped broccoli, thawed

2 cups shredded mozzarella cheese (8 oz.)

1 (9-inch) unbaked pie shell

1 Heat oven to 350°F. In medium skillet, cook onion and bell pepper over medium-high heat 3 to 5 minutes or until tender. Add garlic; cook 30 seconds. Remove from heat; set aside.

2 Break up tofu. In food processor, combine tofu, mustard, lemon juice, salt, 2 tablespoons Parmesan cheese and egg yolk; process until smooth.

3 In large bowl, combine tofu mixture, broccoli, 1 cup mozzarella cheese, remaining Parmesan cheese and onion-bell pepper mixture; mix well. Place in pie shell. Top with remaining 1 cup mozzarella cheese. Bake 35 to 40 minutes or until crust is brown.

6 servings

VEGETABLE LASAGNA

VEGETABLE LASAGNA

Mari Younkin
Colorado Springs, Colorado

12 large lasagna noodles

3 tablespoons olive oil

2 large carrots, sliced

1 cup sliced fresh mushrooms

½ cup diced onions

½ cup diced celery

1 garlic clove, chopped

1 small yellow squash, sliced

1 small green squash, sliced

1 (10-oz.) pkg. chopped frozen spinach,
thawed, drained, squeezed dry

10 to 12 broccoli florets

24 oz. cottage cheese

2 (8-oz.) pkg. shredded Italian four-cheese
cheese blend

8 cups spaghetti sauce with pesto

1 cup freshly grated Parmesan cheese (4 oz.)

1 Cook lasagna noodles according to package directions. Drain; keep noodles separated by placing each on piece of plastic wrap.

2 Heat oven to 350°F. Spray 13x9-inch pan with nonstick cooking spray. In large skillet, heat oil over medium-high heat until hot. Add carrots, mushrooms, onions, celery, garlic and yellow and green squash; sauté 10 to 12 minutes or until tender. Add spinach; reduce heat to low. Place broccoli on top of mixture; cover. Simmer 6 to 8 minutes or until broccoli is tender.

3 In medium bowl, combine cottage cheese and 8 oz. Italian cheese blend; mix well. Set aside. In medium saucepan, heat spaghetti sauce over low heat. Pour 3 cups sauce into pan. Place 4 lasagna noodles over sauce; spread cottage cheese mixture over noodles. Layer with 4 noodles; cover with 2 cups sauce. Spoon vegetable mixture over sauce using slotted spoon. Layer with remaining 4 noodles; top with remaining 3 cups sauce.

4 Bake, uncovered, 45 to 60 minutes. Turn oven off; sprinkle dish with remaining 8 oz. Italian cheese blend. Leave in oven 10 to 15 minutes or until cheese is melted. Remove from oven; cool 20 minutes. Sprinkle with Parmesan cheese.

12 servings

PENNE WITH VODKA

Lorraine Terra
Brooklyn, New York

1 (1-lb.) pkg. penne

2 tablespoons butter

½ cup olive oil

1 large onion, finely chopped

6 to 8 slices aged ham (such as prosciutto),
finely chopped

2 (28-oz.) cans crushed tomatoes

½ cup vodka

½ teaspoon crushed red pepper

2 tablespoons sugar

Salt

Freshly ground pepper

2 cups heavy cream

1 Cook penne according to package directions.

2 In large saucepan, heat butter and olive oil over medium-high heat. When butter has melted, add onion and ham; sauté 3 to 5 minutes or until onion is transparent. Add tomatoes; simmer 15 minutes. Add vodka and red pepper; simmer 10 to 15 minutes. Stir in sugar, salt and pepper. Add cream; simmer 20 to 30 minutes. Serve sauce over penne.

6 to 8 servings

GREEK SPINACH-CHEESE PIE

James Christopoulos
Alexandria, Virginia

1½ lb. frozen spinach, thawed

6 eggs

1 medium onion, diced

1 lb. feta cheese, crumbled

Salt

½ to 1 cup butter, melted

1 (1-lb.) box frozen phyllo dough, thawed

1 Heat oven to 350°F. Squeeze spinach to remove excess moisture. In medium bowl, combine spinach, eggs, onion and cheese; mix well. Season with salt.

2 Brush bottom of 13x9-inch pan with butter. Layer 8 to 10 sheets phyllo in bottom of pan, brushing each layer with butter. (If necessary, trim phyllo to fit pan.) Add spinach mixture; spread evenly to cover bottom. Layer with 8 to 10 sheets phyllo, brushing each layer with butter. Gently score top layers of phyllo to form square-, rectangular- or diamond-shaped pieces.

3 Bake 35 to 40 minutes or until top is golden brown, or until phyllo shrinks and can be shaken from side to side in pan. Cool on wire rack 30 minutes.

12 servings

FRUITED TOFU CURRY

Kimberly Antal
Longmeadow, Massachusetts

½ cup dried apricots, chopped

½ cup fresh orange juice

¼ cup raisins

¼ cup golden raisins

½ cup fresh apple juice

¾ cup mango chutney

¼ cup apple cider vinegar

2½ tablespoons freshly grated ginger

1 teaspoon dry mustard

¼ teaspoon ground cloves

¼ teaspoon cardamom

2 tablespoons canola oil

1 lb. firm tofu, cut into small cubes

2 cups thinly sliced carrots

1 parsnip, thinly sliced

¼ cup chopped onions

6 to 8 green onions, (green part only) very thinly sliced

½ cup slivered almonds, toasted

¼ cup coconut

1 banana, halved lengthwise, thinly sliced

1 In small bowl, soak apricots in orange juice 15 minutes. In another small bowl, soak raisins in apple juice 15 minutes. Drain, reserving juices.

2 Meanwhile, in another small bowl, combine chutney, vinegar, ginger, mustard, cloves and cardamom; mix well.

3 Heat 1 tablespoon oil in large skillet over medium-high heat until hot. Add tofu; stir-fry 6 to 8 minutes or until light brown. Remove from pan; keep warm.

4 In same skillet, heat remaining 1 tablespoon oil over medium-high heat until hot. Add carrots, parsnip and chopped onions; sauté 4 to 6 minutes or until crisp-tender. Add apricots and raisins. (If mixture seems too thick, thin with reserved fruit juices.) Reduce heat to medium. Gently stir in tofu; stir-fry an additional 3 to 4 minutes or until heated through. Stir in chutney mixture; cook about 1 minute. Remove from heat.

5 Stir in green onions. Pour mixture into shallow serving bowl; sprinkle with almonds and coconut. Garnish edges with banana slices. Serve over white or brown basmati rice.

6 servings

SPINACH FRITTATA

Lynne Hudson
Chesapeake, Virginia

1 tablespoon olive oil

1 tablespoon chopped shallots

½ to 1 teaspoon chopped garlic

1 cup spinach leaves, stems removed, torn into bite-size pieces

2 eggs

Salt

Freshly ground pepper

1 to 2 tablespoons shredded Gruyère cheese

1 In small skillet, heat oil over medium heat until hot. Add shallots and garlic; sauté 1 minute. Add spinach; sauté 2 minutes, stirring occasionally.

2 In small bowl, beat eggs until frothy. Sprinkle with salt and pepper. Add to spinach mixture; stir to evenly spread spinach. Sprinkle cheese over top of egg mixture. Cook 2 to 4 minutes, turning once.

1 frittata

POMODORO SAUCE FOR PASTA

Richard Rands
Woodland Hills, California

3 tablespoons olive oil

1 small onion, finely chopped

4 lb. plum tomatoes, seeded

4 garlic cloves, minced

1½ teaspoons salt

½ teaspoon freshly ground pepper

¼ cup finely chopped fresh basil

In large saucepan, heat oil over medium heat until hot. Add onion; sauté 2 to 3 minutes or until transparent. Add tomatoes, garlic, salt and pepper. Reduce heat to medium-low; cover and simmer 20 minutes, stirring frequently. Remove from heat. Stir in basil. Serve with pasta or chicken.

4 cups

PASTA PORTOBELLO

Sharon O'Connell
Milwaukee, Wisconsin

2 cups farfalle (bow-tie pasta)

1 tablespoon olive oil

2 garlic cloves, minced

2 cups sliced portobello mushrooms

2 tablespoons dry sherry

1 (16-oz.) bag frozen broccoli, thawed, steamed to crisp-tender

2 tablespoons chopped fresh basil

Salt

Freshly ground pepper

½ to ¾ cup shredded Parmesan cheese (2 to 3 oz.)

1 Prepare farfalle according to package directions. Drain.

2 In large skillet, heat oil over medium heat until hot. Add garlic; sauté 1 minute. Add mushrooms; cook 6 to 8 minutes or until mushrooms are tender and slightly brown. Add sherry; remove from heat. Scrape bottom of pan to remove any brown bits.

3 Place farfalle in large bowl. Add mushroom-garlic mixture, broccoli, basil, salt and pepper. Top with cheese.

4 servings

CAULIFLOWER CURRY WITH POTATOES AND PEAS

Arvinda Chauhan
Oakville, Ontario

2 to 3 tablespoons vegetable oil

½ teaspoon mustard

½ teaspoon cumin seeds

2 medium russet potatoes, cubed

½ medium cauliflower, cut into small pieces

1 cup peas

2 teaspoons ground cumin

1 teaspoon salt

½ teaspoon chili powder

½ teaspoon turmeric

½ teaspoon garam masala

Chopped fresh coriander

1 In large saucepan, heat oil over medium-high heat until hot. Add mustard and cumin seeds; cover. Fry until seeds sizzle.

2 Add potatoes, cauliflower, peas, cumin, salt, chili powder and turmeric; fry until all spices are blended. Reduce heat to low; cook, covered, 15 minutes or until potatoes are tender.

3 Place in serving dish. Garnish with garam masala and coriander.

5 cups

BOW-TIE PASTA WITH ROASTED VEGETABLES

Priscilla Migliore
Sherman Oaks, California

12 oz. farfalle (bow-tie pasta)

1 red bell pepper, seeded, quartered

1 yellow bell pepper, seeded, quartered

1 green bell pepper, seeded, quartered

2 yellow squash, cut into ½-inch coins

2 green Italian squash, cut into ½-inch slices

1 yellow onion, cut into ½-inch wedges

1 small eggplant, trimmed, cut into 1-inch chunks, halved

2 to 3 garlic cloves, halved

¼ cup extra-virgin olive oil

¼ cup finely chopped Italian parsley

1 tablespoon chopped fresh basil

Salt

Freshly ground pepper

2 tablespoons freshly grated Parmesan cheese

1 Heat oven to 400°F. Cook farfalle according to package directions. Reserve ½ cup cooking water.

2 Cut bell peppers into ½-inch-wide strips. In large roasting pan, combine peppers, yellow squash, Italian squash, onion, eggplant and garlic; add olive oil. Toss to coat. Bake 40 minutes or until brown and tender, turning often. Add 2 tablespoons parsley, ½ tablespoon basil, salt and pepper; mix well.

3 In large bowl, combine pasta, reserved cooking liquid, vegetables and cheese. Sprinkle with remaining 2 tablespoons parsley and ½ tablespoon basil.

6 servings

BOW-TIE PASTA WITH ROASTED VEGETABLES

FRENCH ONION TORTE

Jean McCormick
Deep Park, New York

1 (9-inch) unbaked pie shell

1½ tablespoons olive oil

2 large Spanish onions, cut into ½-inch slices, separated (about 2 cups)

1 teaspoon sugar

½ teaspoon salt

⅛ teaspoon freshly ground pepper

3 eggs

½ teaspoon herbes de Provence

¼ cup heavy cream

1 Heat oven to 400°F. Using fork, poke holes in bottom of pie shell. Bake 15 minutes. Remove from oven; place on baking sheet. Do not turn oven off.

2 In large skillet, heat oil over medium-high heat until hot. Add onions, sugar, salt and pepper; cook 7 minutes or until onions are golden brown and caramelized. Remove onions from skillet; cool to room temperature.

3 In medium bowl, combine eggs, herbes de Provence and cream; mix until combined. Stir in cooled onions. Pour mixture into pie shell. Bake pie 20 to 25 minutes or until toothpick inserted near center comes out clean. Serve warm.

6 servings

MUSHROOM AND SOUR CREAM PIE

Marjorie Cook
Falls Church, Virginia

3 tablespoons butter

½ lb. small mushrooms, sliced

½ cup chopped onions

1 teaspoon all-purpose flour

¼ teaspoon paprika

Salt

Freshly ground pepper

1 (9-inch) pie shell

3 eggs, beaten

1 cup sour cream

2 tablespoons chopped fresh parsley

¼ cup freshly grated Parmesan cheese (1 oz.)

1 Heat oven to 350°F. In large skillet, melt butter over medium-high heat. Add mushrooms and onions; sauté 4 to 5 minutes or until onions are transparent. Add flour, paprika, salt and pepper; mix well. Pour into pie shell.

2 In medium bowl, combine eggs, sour cream, parsley and cheese; mix well. Pour over mushroom mixture. Bake 30 to 35 minutes or until filling is set. Let cool on wire rack 5 minutes.

6 to 8 servings

EGGPLANT-STUFFED RAVIOLI

Barbara Williams
Pumxsy, Pennsylvania

SAUCE

2 tablespoons olive oil

1 tablespoon minced garlic

1 (28-oz.) can crushed tomatoes

2 tablespoons sugar

1 teaspoon freshly ground pepper

$\frac{1}{2}$ teaspoon salt

$\frac{1}{2}$ cup chopped fresh parsley

$\frac{1}{2}$ cup chopped fresh basil

FILLING

2 tablespoons olive oil

1 small eggplant, unpeeled, chopped into $\frac{1}{4}$-inch cubes

2 large garlic cloves, minced

$\frac{1}{4}$ cup plus 1 tablespoon chopped fresh parsley

$\frac{1}{4}$ cup chopped fresh basil

$\frac{3}{4}$ teaspoon salt

$\frac{3}{4}$ teaspoon freshly ground pepper

1 (8-oz.) container ricotta cheese

1 egg, beaten

$\frac{1}{4}$ cup freshly grated Romano cheese (1 oz.)

$\frac{1}{4}$ cup shredded mozzarella cheese (1 oz.)

RAVIOLI

1 (12-oz.) pkg. wonton skins

1 egg, beaten

1 In large saucepan, heat 2 tablespoons oil over medium-high heat until hot. Add 1 tablespoon garlic; sauté 1 minute. Reduce heat to low. Add tomatoes, sugar, 1 teaspoon pepper, $\frac{1}{2}$ teaspoon salt, $\frac{1}{2}$ cup parsley and $\frac{1}{2}$ cup basil; simmer, loosely covered, 1 hour.

2 In large skillet, heat 2 tablespoons oil over medium heat until hot. Add eggplant, 2 garlic cloves, $\frac{1}{4}$ cup parsley, $\frac{1}{4}$ cup basil, and $\frac{1}{2}$ teaspoon each of the salt and pepper; sauté 10 to 12 minutes or until eggplant is tender, stirring occasionally. Remove from heat; let cool. Drain well. Set aside.

3 In large bowl, combine ricotta cheese, 1 egg, Romano cheese, mozzarella cheese, 1 tablespoon parsley, and $\frac{1}{4}$ teaspoon each of the salt and pepper; mix well. Add eggplant mixture to cheese mixture; mix well.

4 Place 1 wonton skin on clean plate; brush $\frac{1}{4}$ inch around edges with egg. Place 1 tablespoon filling in center of skin; cover with 1 wonton skin. Press edges to seal; set aside. Repeat with remaining skins and filling. Place assembled ravioli in single layers on waxed paper to prevent sticking.

5 In large pot, bring 4 quarts water to a boil. Add ravioli (avoid crowding together); cook without stirring 2 to 4 minutes or until ravioli is tender when cut with fork and filling is cooked. With slotted spoon, remove ravioli and arrange on serving platter. Serve with sauce.

6 to 8 servings

THREE CHEESE TORTELLINI

Laurianne Rembisz
Midlothian, Virginia

2 (9-oz.) pkg. cheese tortellini

½ cup butter

1 lb. mushrooms, diced

1 onion, chopped

2 garlic cloves, minced

1 (8-oz.) pkg. cream cheese, cut up

¼ cup all-purpose flour

1¾ cups whole milk

1 tablespoon finely chopped parsley

1 (16-oz.) jar spaghetti sauce

1 cup grated mozzarella cheese (4 oz.)

1 Heat oven to 375°F. Spray 2-quart casserole with nonstick cooking spray. Cook tortellini according to package directions.

2 In large skillet, melt butter over medium-high heat. Add mushrooms, onion and garlic; sauté 10 minutes or until mushrooms are tender. Add cream cheese, flour and milk; cook 5 minutes or until cheese is melted, stirring occasionally.

3 Add tortellini and parsley to cream cheese mixture; mix well. Spread mixture evenly in casserole; pour spaghetti sauce over top. Sprinkle with mozzarella cheese. Bake, uncovered, 30 to 40 minutes.

6 servings

PASTA WITH SWISS CHARD AND SMOKED GOUDA

Joan Deady
San Francisco, California

1 (1-lb.) pkg. fettuccine

2 tablespoons olive oil

2 garlic cloves, minced

16 cups coarsely chopped Swiss chard (about 2 bunches)

2 tomatoes, chopped

½ cup pine nuts

¼ teaspoon freshly ground pepper

½ lb. smoked Gouda cheese, grated

1 Cook fettuccine according to package directions.

2 In large saucepan, heat oil over medium heat. Add garlic; sauté 1 minute. Add chard; sauté 5 minutes or until wilted. Stir in tomatoes, nuts and pepper.

3 Sprinkle fettuccine with cheese; top with chard mixture.

6 to 8 servings

EGGS McGLASSON

Jeff and Abby Wilson
Minneapolis, Minnesota

¼ cup butter

3 tablespoons all-purpose flour

¼ teaspoon salt

⅛ teaspoon freshly ground pepper

1 cup milk

1 tablespoon fresh lemon juice

8 hard-cooked eggs, coarsely chopped

12 English muffins, split, toasted, buttered

1 In large saucepan, melt butter over low heat. Stir in flour, salt and pepper. Cook 1 to 2 minutes or until smooth and bubbly. Remove from heat; stir in milk and lemon juice. Return to heat. Increase heat to medium. Bring to a boil; boil 1 minute, stirring constantly. Carefully fold in eggs.

2 Spoon mixture over muffins; season with salt and pepper.

6 servings

Desserts

BUTTERMILK RAISIN PIE

Albin Schulz
Appleton, Minnesota

MERINGUE

4 egg whites

½ teaspoon cream of tartar

½ cup sugar

FILLING

⅔ cup sugar

2 tablespoons cornstarch

½ teaspoon cinnamon

¼ teaspoon ground cloves

¼ teaspoon salt

4 egg yolks

1 cup buttermilk or sour cream

1½ cups raisins

1 cup water

1 teaspoon vanilla

1 (9-inch) pie shell

1 Heat oven to 350°F. In large bowl, beat egg whites at high speed 1 minute or until soft peaks form. Add cream of tartar; beat until stiff. Slowly add ½ cup sugar; beat until stiff. Set aside.

2 In medium bowl, combine ⅔ cup sugar, cornstarch, cinnamon, cloves and salt; mix well. Set aside. In small bowl, combine egg yolks and buttermilk; mix well. Slowly mix in cornstarch mixture.

3 In medium saucepan, combine raisins and water; bring to a boil over medium heat. Add cornstarch mixture and vanilla; mix well. Return to a boil; reduce heat to medium-low. Cook 2 minutes, stirring constantly.

4 Pour raisin mixture into pie shell. Top with egg white mixture. Bake 15 minutes or until meringue is lightly browned.

1 (9-inch) pie

CHOCOLATE BOX CAKE WITH STRAWBERRIES AND CREAM

Rosemary Siewert
Apple Valley, Minnesota

6 oz. semisweet chocolate, chopped

1 tablespoon shortening

2 (3-oz.) pkg. cream cheese, softened

¼ cup butter

1½ cups powdered sugar

⅓ cup unsweetened cocoa

2 tablespoons milk

1 teaspoon vanilla

2½ cups heavy cream

4 cups strawberries, halved

Mint leaves

1 Line 9-inch square cake pan with aluminum foil; smooth out wrinkles.

2 In small saucepan, melt chocolate and shortening over low heat until smooth, stirring frequently. Pour into pan; swirl around sides and bottom of pan to cover evenly, keeping edges as even as possible. Refrigerate 1 minute; swirl chocolate again around inside of pan. Refrigerate 30 minutes or until firm.

3 To prepare filling, in large bowl, beat cream cheese and butter at medium speed until smooth. Add sugar, cocoa, milk and vanilla; beat until fluffy.

4 In small bowl, beat 1½ cups cream until stiff. Fold into cream cheese mixture.

5 Remove foil and chocolate from pan; peel foil from chocolate. Place chocolate box on serving platter. Spread cream cheese mixture evenly in chocolate box. Refrigerate 2 to 3 hours or until filling is chilled and firm.

6 In another small bowl, beat remaining 1 cup cream at medium speed until stiff peaks form. Spoon into pastry bag fitted with large rosette tip. Pipe cream in 1-inch-wide border around chocolate box. Place strawberries on top of filling. Garnish with mint leaves.

8 servings

LEMON PIE

Elizabeth Long
West Hollywood, California

1 (8-inch) unbaked pie shell

3 egg whites

1/2 cup sugar

FILLING

3 1/2 tablespoons cornstarch

3 tablespoons cold water

3/4 cup sugar

3/4 cup boiling water

3 egg yolks

1/4 cup fresh lemon juice

1 tablespoon grated lemon peel

2 tablespoons butter

1 cup whipping cream

2 tablespoons powdered sugar

1 banana, mashed

1 Bake pie shell according to package directions. Cool.

2 In small bowl, beat egg whites at high speed until soft peaks form. With mixer running, add 1/2 cup sugar 1 tablespoon at a time until stiff peaks form. Spread over bottom and up sides of pie shell. Bake at 250°F for 30 minutes or until meringue is golden. Remove from oven; cool completely.

3 In another small bowl, mix together cornstarch and cold water. In heavy medium saucepan, combine 3/4 cup sugar, cornstarch mixture and boiling water. Cook over medium heat until mixture has thickened.

4 In another small bowl, whisk together egg yolks, lemon juice and lemon peel. Slowly whisk into cornstarch mixture. Cook over low heat about 5 minutes, stirring constantly. Remove from heat; place butter on top of egg yolk mixture. Let butter melt; stir into egg yolk mixture. Pour into cooled meringue shell.

5 In medium bowl, beat cream and powdered sugar at high speed. Fold banana into cream mixture; spread over top of pie.

6 servings

RED BEET CHOCOLATE CAKE

Elizabeth Long
West Hollywood, California

4 cups water

4 medium beets

1 1/2 cups sugar

3 eggs

1 cup vegetable oil

2 (1-oz.) squares unsweetened chocolate

1 3/4 cup all-purpose flour

1 1/2 teaspoons baking soda

1/2 teaspoon salt

FROSTING

2 tablespoons unsweetened cocoa

2 tablespoons butter

2 tablespoons water

1 tablespoon light corn syrup

1 cup powdered sugar

1 Heat oven to 350°F. Spray 13x9-inch pan with nonstick cooking spray; lightly flour. In medium saucepan, bring 4 cups water to a boil. Add beets; cook until soft. Drain; mash beets.

2 In large bowl, beat sugar and eggs. Add oil and mashed beets; mix well.

3 In small saucepan, melt chocolate over low heat. Stir into beet mixture.

4 In medium bowl, sift together flour, baking soda and salt. Stir into beet mixture; pour into pan. Bake 20 to 25 minutes or until toothpick inserted near center comes out clean. Cool on wire rack until completely cool.

5 To make frosting, in another small saucepan, combine cocoa, butter, 2 tablespoons water and corn syrup; bring to a boil. Remove from heat; stir in powdered sugar. Frost top of cake.

12 servings

NO-BAKE MASCARPONE KEY LIME PIE

NO-BAKE MASCARPONE KEY LIME PIE

Carolyn Lucarelli
State College, Pennsylvania

CRUST

1 1/4 cups graham-cracker crumbs

1 tablespoon unsalted butter, melted

2 tablespoons canola oil

2 tablespoons honey

1 tablespoon water

FILLING

1 cup reduced-fat sour cream

1/2 cup mascarpone cheese

1/2 cup nonfat yogurt cheese*

1 (14-oz.) can nonfat sweetened condensed skimmed milk

1/3 cup Key lime juice**

1 Spray 9-inch pie pan with nonstick cooking spray. In food processor, combine graham-cracker crumbs, butter, oil, honey and water; pulse until crumbs are moistened and hold together well. Add additional water if needed. Press mixture evenly into bottom and up sides of pan. Cover; refrigerate at least 2 hours.

2 To make filling, in large bowl, combine sour cream, mascarpone cheese, nonfat yogurt cheese, milk and lime juice; beat until well combined and smooth. Pour mixture into chilled crust; smooth top with spatula. Refrigerate 2 hours. If desired, garnish with fresh lime slices.

TIPS *To make yogurt cheese, drain 1 1/4 cups non-fat plain yogurt through cheesecloth-lined colander set over bowl. Let drain at least 12 hours in refrigerator. Discard whey that collects in bottom of bowl, or save for another use.

**If you can't find Key lime juice, substitute fresh lime juice.

8 servings

LEMON YOGURT CAKE

Daphine Smith
Baytown, Texas

3 cups all-purpose flour

1 teaspoon baking soda

1/2 teaspoon salt

6 eggs, separated

2 cups sugar

1 cup butter

2 teaspoons grated lemon peel

1/2 teaspoon lemon extract

1 cup plain yogurt

1 Heat oven to 325°F. Line 10-inch tube pan with parchment paper; grease and flour.

2 In medium bowl, combine flour, baking soda and salt; set aside. In small bowl, whisk egg whites until soft peaks form; gradually add 1/2 cup sugar, beating until mixture is stiff.

3 In large bowl, beat butter until creamy. Add remaining 1 1/2 cups sugar; beat until fluffy. Add egg yolks, lemon peel and lemon extract; beat until thick and pale yellow. Add flour mixture alternately with yogurt to butter mixture until blended. Fold in egg white mixture. Pour into tube pan.

4 Bake 45 to 50 minutes or until toothpick inserted near center comes out clean. Cool in pan 15 minutes; invert onto wire rack to finish cooling.

12 to 16 servings

KING'S KRAZE WITH BOILED CUSTARD

Virginia McDougall
Escondido, California

CAKE

1 cup finely chopped pitted dates

1 cup chopped pecans

1 cup sugar

3 tablespoons fresh bread crumbs

2 tablespoons all-purpose flour

1 teaspoon baking powder

3 tablespoons milk

3 egg whites

CUSTARD

1 tablespoon cornstarch

3 egg yolks

¼ cup sugar

2 cups hot milk

1 teaspoon vanilla

⅛ teaspoon salt

1 Heat oven to 350°F. In medium bowl, combine dates, pecans, 1 cup sugar, bread crumbs, flour, baking powder, 3 tablespoons milk and egg whites; mix well. Place in ungreased 9x5-inch loaf pan. Bake 40 minutes or until browned; cool.

2 To make custard, in small saucepan, combine cornstarch, egg yolks and ¼ cup sugar; beat well. Stir in hot milk, vanilla and salt. Cook over low heat 5 minutes or just until set, stirring constantly. Remove from heat; cool. Pour over filling.

12 servings

ENGLISH TRIFLE

Bernadette Lindholm
Minneapolis, Minnesota

2 (3-oz.) pkg. ladyfingers

2 tablespoons raspberry jam

6 coconut macaroons*

¼ cup brandy

1 pkg. vanilla pudding mix**

2 cups milk

¼ cup dry sherry

1 cup whipping cream

1 teaspoon vanilla

1 banana, sliced

1 pint fresh strawberries, sliced

1 cup fresh blueberries

2 (8¼-oz.) cans pineapple chunks, drained

3 oz. maraschino cherries, drained

1 cup toasted almonds***

1 Place half of ladyfingers on baking sheet; spread with thin layer of jam. In medium bowl, break jam-coated ladyfingers and macaroons into bite-size pieces with fork. Sprinkle with brandy. Let sit 1 hour.

2 Meanwhile, in medium saucepan, combine pudding mix and milk. Prepare pudding according to package directions; cool. Add sherry to cooled pudding; mix well.

3 In medium bowl, beat cream and vanilla at high speed until stiff.

4 Line sides of 2½-quart casserole with remaining half of ladyfingers. Layer with half each of the macaroon mixture, banana, strawberries, blueberries, pineapple, cherries, almonds and vanilla cream. Repeat with remaining half of macaroon mixture, banana, strawberries, blueberries, pineapple and vanilla cream. Top with cherries and almonds.

TIPS * If macaroons are unavailable, substitute 1 (3-oz.) pkg. ladyfingers.

** Do not use instant pudding.

***To toast almonds, spread on baking sheet; bake at 375°F for 4 to 7 minutes or until lightly browned.

12 to 15 servings

LEMON-BLUEBERRY CHEESECAKE

Mulu Lucas
Seattle, Washington

CRUST

2 cups finely crushed graham crackers

½ cup sifted powdered sugar

½ cup butter, melted

FILLING

3 (8-oz.) pkg. cream cheese, softened

1 (14-oz.) can sweetened condensed milk

4 eggs

1 teaspoon vanilla

2 cups blueberries

½ cup fresh lemon juice

1 tablespoon grated lemon peel

½ teaspoon lemon extract

1 Heat oven to 325°F. In large bowl, combine graham crackers and powdered sugar; stir in butter. Press evenly into bottom and 1 inch up sides of 10-inch springform pan. Wrap bottom of pan with aluminum foil. Set aside.

2 In large bowl, beat cream cheese and condensed milk at medium speed until smooth and creamy. Add eggs one at a time, beating just until combined. Add vanilla; beat just until well blended and smooth.

3 Pour half of batter into medium bowl; fold in blueberries. Set aside.

4 To remaining half of cream cheese mixture, add lemon juice, lemon peel and lemon extract; beat until combined.

5 Pour blueberry-cream cheese mixture into springform pan. Top with lemon-cream cheese mixture.

6 Place springform pan in large shallow roasting pan or broiler pan. Fill with ½ inch hot water.

7 Bake 50 to 60 minutes or until center edges are puffed and top looks dull and is dry to the touch. Center should be less set than edges and will move when pan is tapped. It should not ripple as if liquid. Turn oven off; leave cheesecake in oven 10 to 15 minutes.

8 Remove from oven. Let stand in water bath 20 to 30 minutes. Remove from water bath; cool completely on wire rack. Cover; refrigerate at least 4 hours.

16 servings

INDIVIDUAL TIRAMISU DESSERTS

Cecelia Rooney
Point Pleasant, New Jersey

2 (8-oz.) pkg. cream cheese, softened

⅔ cup sugar

¼ cup marsala wine

2 teaspoons vanilla

2 cups whipping cream, whipped

1 cup strong coffee, chilled

2 tablespoons almond liqueur

24 ladyfingers, cut horizontally, then vertically (6 oz.)

1 cup English toffee bits

1 In large bowl, beat cream cheese and sugar until soft and creamy. Stir in wine and vanilla. Fold in whipping cream.

2 In small bowl, combine coffee and liqueur.

3 To assemble, place 4 ladyfinger pieces in each of 8 large wine glasses. Drizzle each with 2 teaspoons coffee mixture; top each with ¼ cup cream cheese mixture and 2 tablespoons toffee bits. Repeat layering two more times. Cover; refrigerate 2 hours.

8 desserts

SQUASH AND WALNUT PIE

Kimberly Antal
Longmeadow, Massachusetts

PIE

2 eggs, beaten

$\frac{1}{2}$ cup sugar

$\frac{1}{2}$ cup packed brown sugar

1 tablespoon all-purpose flour

$1\frac{1}{4}$ teaspoons cinnamon

$\frac{1}{2}$ teaspoon nutmeg

$\frac{1}{2}$ teaspoon ginger

2 cups cooked mashed winter squash

1 (14-oz.) can evaporated milk

1 (10-inch) unbaked pie shell

TOPPING

2 tablespoons unsalted butter, softened

$\frac{1}{4}$ cup packed brown sugar

1 tablespoon grated orange peel

$\frac{3}{4}$ cup coarsely chopped walnuts

CREAM

1 cup whipping cream

2 tablespoons powdered sugar

1 Heat oven to 450°F. In large bowl, combine eggs, sugar, $\frac{1}{2}$ cup brown sugar, flour, cinnamon, nutmeg and ginger; mix well. Mix in squash. Slowly stir in milk; mix well. Place mixture in pie shell.

2 In small bowl, combine butter, $\frac{1}{4}$ cup brown sugar, orange rind and walnuts; mix well. Sprinkle over squash mixture. Place foil over pie edges. Bake 10 minutes. Reduce oven temperature to 350°F; bake an additional 45 to 55 minutes or until knife inserted near center of pie comes out clean. Cool on wire rack.

3 To make cream, in small bowl beat cream and powdered sugar until stiff. Serve with pie. Dust with nutmeg, if desired.

6 to 8 servings

BANANAS FOSTER

Clara Edenfield
Franklinton, California

4 medium firm bananas

$\frac{1}{2}$ cup packed brown sugar

$\frac{1}{4}$ cup butter

Dash cinnamon

$\frac{1}{3}$ cup light rum

8 scoops coffee or vanilla ice cream

1 Cut bananas in half lengthwise, then crosswise.

2 In large skillet, heat brown sugar and butter over medium heat until sugar is melted. Cook 2 minutes or until slightly thickened, stirring constantly. Add bananas; cook 1 to 2 minutes or until bananas are heated and glazed. Sprinkle lightly with cinnamon. Add rum. Using long match, carefully light rum. Spoon liquid over bananas 1 minute or until flames die out. Remove from heat.

3 Serve warm over ice cream.

4 servings

TEXAS PECAN PIE

Elaine Welsh
Rowlett, Texas

FILLING

4 eggs

$1\frac{1}{4}$ cups light corn syrup

$\frac{1}{2}$ cup sugar

2 tablespoons butter

2 teaspoons vanilla

$1\frac{1}{4}$ cups pecan pieces

Pinch salt

CRUST

1 (10-inch) unbaked pie shell

Heat oven to 350°F. In medium bowl, combine eggs, corn syrup, sugar, butter, vanilla, pecans and salt. Pour into shell. Bake 55 to 60 minutes or until set. Cool on wire rack.

8 servings

BANANAS FOSTER

NO-BAKE FRESH PEACH PIE

Vicki Fisher
Union, South Carolina

PIE

¾ cup sugar

4 oz. cream cheese

1 (9-inch) baked pie shell

2 to 3 fresh peaches, sliced

1½ tablespoons cornstarch

½ cup water

2 tablespoons peach-flavored gelatin

TOPPING

1 cup heavy cream

2 tablespoons powdered sugar

1 teaspoon vanilla

1 In medium bowl, beat ¼ cup sugar and cream cheese at medium speed until smooth. Spread in bottom of pie shell. Layer with peaches.

2 In small saucepan, combine remaining ½ cup sugar and cornstarch; mix well. Stir in water. Bring mixture to a boil over medium-low heat. Stir in gelatin. Pour over peaches in shell.

3 In small bowl, beat cream, sugar and vanilla until stiff. Serve with pie.

1 (9-inch) pie

SOUR CREAM CARROT CAKE

Joan Deady
San Francisco, California

1½ cups packed brown sugar

1¼ cups all-purpose flour

1 cup whole wheat flour

2 teaspoons baking soda

2 teaspoons cinnamon

½ teaspoon salt

4 eggs

¾ cup safflower oil

1 teaspoon vanilla

1 teaspoon fresh lemon juice

1 cup nonfat sour cream

2 cups grated carrots

¾ cup chopped walnuts

FROSTING

2 (8-oz.) pkg. light cream cheese, softened

2 cups powdered sugar

1 teaspoon vanilla

1 Heat oven to 350°F. Grease 13x9-inch pan. In large bowl, combine brown sugar, all-purpose flour, whole wheat flour, baking soda, cinnamon and salt.

2 In small bowl, beat eggs. Add oil, 1 teaspoon vanilla, lemon juice and sour cream; mix well. Add to flour mixture; mix well. Fold in carrots and walnuts. Pour batter into pan. Bake 30 to 40 minutes. Cool on wire rack.

3 To make frosting, in medium bowl, cream together cream cheese, powdered sugar and 1 teaspoon vanilla. Spread over cooled cake.

12 to 15 servings

KIMBERLY'S PEACH-ALMOND STREUSEL PIE

Kimberly Antal
Longmeadow, Massachusetts

PIE

5 cups peeled sliced peaches

2¹⁄₂ tablespoons quick-cooking tapioca

1¹⁄₂ tablespoons cornstarch

3 tablespoons packed brown sugar

2 tablespoons sugar

¹⁄₄ teaspoon cinnamon

¹⁄₄ teaspoon nutmeg

Dash ginger

1 tablespoon fresh lemon juice

1 teaspoon almond extract

1 (9-inch) unbaked pie shell

TOPPING

1 cup whole wheat flour

¹⁄₂ cup packed brown sugar

¹⁄₂ cup butter, softened

¹⁄₄ teaspoon nutmeg

Dash allspice

¹⁄₂ cup blanched slivered almonds, coarsely chopped

1 Heat oven to 425°F. In blender, puree 1 cup peaches.

2 In small bowl, combine 1 cup pureed peaches, tapioca, cornstarch, 3 tablespoons brown sugar, sugar, cinnamon, ¹⁄₄ teaspoon nutmeg, ginger, lemon juice and almond extract; mix well. Let sit 15 minutes. Stir in remaining 4 cups peach slices.

3 In medium bowl, combine flour, ¹⁄₂ cup brown sugar, sugar, butter, ¹⁄₄ teaspoon nutmeg, allspice and almonds; mix well.

4 Place pie shell on baking sheet. Pour peach mixture into shell. Spread topping over peach mixture. Bake 10 minutes. Reduce oven temperature to 350°F; bake an additional 30 to 40 minutes or until bubbly and thickened. If crust is getting too brown, cover edges with foil during last 15 minutes of baking time.

5 Remove from oven; cool on wire rack.

6 to 8 servings

GERMAN APPLE CAKE

Bonnie Bowers
Volcano, California

4 eggs

2 cups vegetable oil

2 cups sugar

2 teaspoons vanilla

4 cups all-purpose flour

4 teaspoons cinnamon

2 teaspoons baking soda

1 teaspoon salt

2 cups chopped walnuts

5 cups tart green apples, coarsely chopped

1 Heat oven to 350°F. Grease 13x9-inch pan. In medium bowl, combine eggs, oil, sugar and vanilla; mix well.

2 In another medium bowl, combine flour, cinnamon, baking soda and salt. Add flour mixture to sugar mixture; stir until combined. Fold in walnuts and apples. Spread mixture in pan. Bake 55 to 60 minutes or until toothpick inserted near center comes out clean.

16 servings

DECADENT DOUBLE-CHOCOLATE LAYER CAKE

DECADENT DOUBLE-CHOCOLATE LAYER CAKE

David Heppner
Brandon, Florida

CAKE

3 oz. semisweet chocolate, finely chopped

1½ cups hot coffee

3 cups sugar

2½ cups all-purpose flour

1½ cups unsweetened cocoa

2 teaspoons baking soda

1¼ teaspoons salt

¾ teaspoon baking powder

3 eggs

¾ cup vegetable oil

1½ cups buttermilk

¾ teaspoon vanilla

GANACHE

1 cup heavy cream

2 tablespoons sugar

2 tablespoons light corn syrup

1 lb. semisweet chocolate, finely chopped

¼ cup unsalted butter, cut up

1 Heat oven to 300°F. Spray 3 (9-inch) round cake pans with nonstick cooking spray. Line bottoms with parchment paper; spray paper. In small bowl, combine 3 oz. chocolate and coffee. Let rest until chocolate is melted and mixture is smooth, stirring occasionally.

2 In large bowl, combine 3 cups sugar, flour, cocoa, baking soda, salt and baking powder; mix well. In another large bowl, beat eggs at medium speed 3 minutes or until slightly thickened and lemon colored. Slowly add oil, buttermilk, vanilla and melted chocolate mixture; beat until well combined. Add sugar mixture; beat just until well combined.

3 Divide batter evenly among cake pans. Bake on middle oven rack 40 to 45 minutes or until toothpick inserted near center comes out clean. Cool completely in pans on wire racks. Invert onto racks. Remove parchment paper; cool completely.

4 In medium saucepan, combine cream, 2 tablespoons sugar and corn syrup; bring to a boil over medium-low heat, whisking until sugar is dissolved. Remove from heat. Add 1 lb. semisweet chocolate; whisk until chocolate is melted. Add butter; whisk until smooth. Place mixture in bowl; cool until spreadable, stirring occasionally.

5 To assemble cake, spread chocolate mixture on top of one cake. Top with second cake; spread top with frosting. Top with third cake; spread top and sides with frosting. (*Cake can be made up to 3 days ahead. Cover and refrigerate. Bring to room temperature before serving.*)

12 servings

BLUEBERRY BUCKLE

Gloria Gluvna
Palmyra, Pennsylvania

FILLING

¾ cup nonfat milk

1 egg

2 cups all-purpose flour

¾ cup sugar

2½ teaspoons baking powder

¾ teaspoon salt

¼ cup shortening

2 cups fresh blueberries, well drained

TOPPING

½ cup sugar

⅓ cup all-purpose flour

½ teaspoon cinnamon

¼ cup butter, softened

1 Heat oven to 375°F. Grease 9-inch square pan.

2 In blender, combine milk, egg, 2 cups flour, ¾ cup sugar, baking powder, salt and shortening. Blend 30 seconds or until mixture is smooth. Pour into pan. Stir in blueberries.

3 In small bowl, combine ½ cup sugar, ⅓ cup flour, cinnamon and butter; mix well. Sprinkle over filling. Bake 45 to 50 minutes or until filling is set.

9 servings

COCOA POUND CAKE

Joanne Scarpone
Clementon, New Jersey

1½ cups butter

3 cups sugar

1 tablespoon vanilla

5 eggs

3 cups all-purpose flour

3 tablespoons unsweetened cocoa

¾ cup club soda

1 Heat oven to 325°F. Grease 10-inch tube pan. In large bowl, beat butter at medium speed 2 minutes or until creamy. Gradually add sugar; beat at medium speed 4 to 5 minutes or until light and fluffy. Add vanilla; mix well. Add eggs one at a time, beating well after each addition.

2 In medium bowl, combine flour and cocoa; mix well. Add to butter mixture; mix well. Fold in soda. Pour into pan; bake 1 hour 15 minutes. Cool in pan 15 minutes. Turn out onto wire rack; cool completely.

16 servings

FUDGE PIE

Reita Morris
Mt. Vernon, Illinois

¾ cup sugar

¼ cup unsweetened cocoa

3 tablespoons all-purpose flour

⅛ teaspoon salt

½ cup butter, melted

3 eggs, warmed*

½ teaspoon vanilla

1 (9-inch) uncooked pie shell

Heat oven to 375°F. In medium bowl, combine sugar, cocoa, flour and salt; mix well. Stir in butter; mix well. Beat in eggs and vanilla. Pour into pie shell. Bake 35 minutes or until toothpick inserted near center comes out clean.

TIP *To warm eggs, place uncracked eggs in a small bowl of warm water several minutes.

1 (8-inch) pie

ALMOND CHEESECAKE

Bonnie Bowers
Volcano, California

CRUST

$1\frac{2}{3}$ cups graham-cracker crumbs

$\frac{1}{2}$ cup finely ground nuts

$\frac{1}{4}$ cup sugar

2 tablespoons wheat germ

2 teaspoons all-purpose flour

$\frac{1}{2}$ cup butter, melted

2 teaspoons vanilla

FILLING

6 (8-oz.) pkg. cream cheese

$1\frac{1}{2}$ cups sugar

6 eggs, lightly beaten

1 tablespoon fresh lemon juice

1 tablespoon vanilla

1 tablespoon almond extract

$\frac{1}{4}$ teaspoon salt

TOPPING

1 (16-oz.) container sour cream

$\frac{3}{4}$ cup sugar

$\frac{3}{4}$ teaspoon almond extract

$\frac{1}{2}$ teaspoon fresh lemon juice

$\frac{1}{8}$ teaspoon salt

1 Heat oven to 350°F. In medium bowl, combine graham-cracker crumbs, nuts, $\frac{1}{4}$ cup sugar, wheat germ, flour, butter and 2 teaspoons vanilla; mix well. Press mixture evenly in bottom and $\frac{3}{4}$ of the way up sides of 10-inch springform pan. Bake 5 minutes; let cool. Turn oven off.

2 In large bowl, beat cream cheese at medium speed until smooth and creamy. Add $1\frac{1}{2}$ cups sugar; beat until smooth. Scrape down bowl and beaters several times. Add eggs, 1 tablespoon lemon juice, 1 tablespoon vanilla, 1 tablespoon almond extract and $\frac{1}{4}$ teaspoon salt; beat at low speed until well blended.

3 Place springform pan on baking sheet; pour batter over crust. Place in oven; bake 65 minutes or until top is golden brown. Center should move slightly when pan is tapped, but should not ripple as if liquid. Remove from oven.

4 In small bowl, combine sour cream, $\frac{3}{4}$ cup sugar, $\frac{3}{4}$ teaspoon almond extract, $\frac{1}{2}$ teaspoon lemon juice and $\frac{1}{8}$ teaspoon salt; blend well. Spread over cheesecake to within $\frac{1}{8}$ inch from edge. Bake an additional 10 minutes; cool on wire rack, away from drafts. Cover; refrigerate overnight.

16 servings

COSMOPOLITAN BREAD PUDDING

Lillian Shimabukuro
Mountain View, Hawaii

2 cups milk

1 cup sugar

$\frac{1}{2}$ cup butter

5 eggs, beaten

1 (1-lb.) loaf day-old sweet bread, cut into 1-inch cubes

1 (21-oz.) can apple pie filling

1 cup raisins

$\frac{1}{2}$ cup chopped macadamia nuts

$\frac{1}{2}$ teaspoon cinnamon

1 Heat oven to 350°F. Spray 13x9-inch pan with nonstick cooking spray. In medium saucepan, combine milk, sugar and butter; heat over medium heat until butter is melted, stirring occasionally. Cool. Whisk in eggs.

2 In large bowl, combine bread and egg mixture; stir until bread is soaked. Pour into pan. Spread pie filling over bread mixture; top with raisins and nuts. Sprinkle with cinnamon. Bake 30 minutes or until set.

12 servings

FRUIT PIZZA

Julie Barker
Shirley, Illinois

CRUST

1 cup butter

1 cup sugar

2 eggs

$\frac{1}{2}$ teaspoon vanilla

$2\frac{3}{4}$ cups all-purpose flour

$\frac{3}{4}$ teaspoon salt

$\frac{1}{2}$ teaspoon baking soda

$\frac{1}{2}$ teaspoon baking powder

FILLING

2 (8-oz.) pkg. cream cheese

$\frac{2}{3}$ cup sugar

1 teaspoon vanilla

TOPPING

Sliced fresh strawberries, pineapple, honeydew melon, star fruit, kiwi, cantaloupe, grapes and/or whole blueberries

2 oz. white chocolate, melted

1 Heat oven to 350°F. Spray 2 (12-inch) pizza pans with nonstick cooking spray.

2 In large bowl, combine butter and 1 cup sugar; beat at medium speed until soft and smooth. Add eggs one at a time, beating well after each addition. Add $\frac{1}{2}$ teaspoon vanilla, flour, salt, baking soda and baking powder; mix well. Press half of dough into each pan. Bake 8 to 10 minutes or until lightly browned; cool. Remove crusts from pans.

3 To make filling, in medium bowl, combine cream cheese, $\frac{2}{3}$ cup sugar and 1 teaspoon vanilla; mix well. Spread $\frac{1}{2}$ of filling over each crust; top with fruit. Drizzle with melted chocolate. Top with toasted slivered almonds, if desired.

2 (12-slice) pizzas

FRUIT PIZZA

APPLE TART

Paula Brady
Burgettstown, Pennsylvania

DOUGH

$\frac{1}{2}$ cup butter

$\frac{1}{2}$ cup sugar

1 egg yolk

1$\frac{1}{2}$ cups all-purpose flour

Pinch salt

$\frac{1}{8}$ teaspoon baking powder

CUSTARD

1 cup milk

Peel of $\frac{1}{2}$ lemon

3 egg yolks

$\frac{1}{4}$ cup sugar

$\frac{1}{4}$ cup all-purpose flour

1$\frac{1}{2}$ teaspoons butter

APPLES

4 medium apples, sliced

$\frac{1}{4}$ cup sugar

$\frac{1}{2}$ teaspoon cinnamon

1 teaspoon lemon juice

$\frac{1}{2}$ cup apple-flavored jelly, melted

1 Heat oven to 350°F. In medium bowl, beat $\frac{1}{2}$ cup butter at medium speed until soft and smooth; gradually beat in $\frac{1}{2}$ cup sugar. Add 1 egg yolk; mix well.

2 In another medium bowl, combine 1$\frac{1}{2}$ cups flour, salt and baking powder; mix well. Stir into butter mixture. With hands, work mixture into ball. Press in bottom and up sides of 10-inch tart pan. Cover and refrigerate.

3 In small saucepan, combine milk and lemon peel; bring to a boil over medium heat. Reduce heat to low; simmer 10 minutes. Remove peel.

4 Place 3 egg yolks in medium saucepan; gradually beat in $\frac{1}{4}$ cup sugar until mixture is pale yellow. Beat in $\frac{1}{4}$ cup flour; gradually add milk. Cook over medium heat until thickened and smooth, stirring constantly. Remove from heat; whisk in 1$\frac{1}{2}$ teaspoons butter. Cool, stirring occasionally.

5 While custard is cooling, place apples in another medium bowl. In small bowl, combine $\frac{1}{4}$ cup sugar, cinnamon and lemon juice; mix well. Pour over apples; stir to coat apples.

6 Remove crust from refrigerator. Spread custard over crust; arrange apple slices in overlapping circles over custard. Bake 1 hour or until crust is well browned. Cool on wire rack. Spoon jelly over apples. Serve at room temperature or chilled.

6 to 8 servings

CARAMEL APPLE CRUNCH PIE

Mary Taylor
Midland, Michigan

CRUST

1 ½ cups sifted all-purpose flour

2 teaspoons sugar

½ teaspoon salt

6 tablespoons unsalted butter, chilled, cut into ½-inch cubes

¼ cup lard, chilled

2 to 3 tablespoons ice water

TOPPING

1 cup all-purpose flour

½ cup butter, chilled

½ cup packed brown sugar

FILLING

½ cup sugar

¼ cup packed brown sugar

¼ cup all-purpose flour

½ teaspoon ground nutmeg

6 cups apples (Jonagold, Granny Smith, Cortland and/or Golden Delicious)

¼ to ½ cup caramel sauce*

3 tablespoons butter

1 In large bowl, combine 1 ½ cups flour, 2 teaspoons sugar and salt; mix well. With pastry blender or two knives, work unsalted butter and lard into flour mixture; blend until butter and lard crumble. Add water 1 tablespoon at a time until dough begins to stick together.

2 Shape dough into flat disk; wrap in plastic wrap. Refrigerate 30 minutes.

3 Heat oven to 400°F. In medium bowl, combine ½ cup flour, ½ cup butter and ½ cup brown sugar. Mix with pastry blender or two knives until mixture crumbles. Set aside.

4 On lightly floured surface, roll out dough to fit 9-inch pie pan; line pan with dough. In another large bowl, combine ½ cup sugar, ¼ cup brown sugar, ¼ cup flour, nutmeg and apples; pour into crust. Cover with caramel sauce; dot with 3 tablespoons butter. Sprinkle with topping mixture.

5 Bake 50 minutes or until apples are tender.

TIP *The caramel used for dipping apples works well in this recipe.

8 to 10 servings

APPLE CRISP PIE

Sandra Gregg
Palm Harbor, Florida

1 cup all-purpose flour

1 cup sugar

1 teaspoon baking soda

½ teaspoon salt

1 ¼ teaspoons cinnamon

¼ plus ⅛ teaspoon nutmeg

1 egg, beaten

3 lb. tart green apples, cut into eighths

⅓ cup butter, melted

1 Heat oven to 350°F. Grease 9-inch pie pan. In large bowl, combine flour, sugar, baking soda, salt, ¼ teaspoon of the cinnamon and ⅛ teaspoon of the nutmeg. With hands or fork, mix in egg until mixture crumbles. Press mixture into pan.

2 Add apples; sprinkle with remaining 1 teaspoon cinnamon and ¼ teaspoon remaining nutmeg. Pour butter over apples and flour mixture. Bake 1 hour or until topping is crispy and browned.

8 servings

CHOCOLATE-DIPPED STRAWBERRY TART

Cindy Emmans
Ellensburg, Washington

CRUST

1 cup all-purpose flour

3 tablespoons packed brown sugar

Dash salt

6 tablespoons butter, chilled, cut up

1 egg yolk

1 tablespoon water

PASTRY CREAM

¼ cup sugar

2 tablespoons all-purpose flour

3 egg yolks

¾ cup milk

1 tablespoon butter

¼ teaspoon almond extract

CHOCOLATE LAYER

3 oz. bittersweet chocolate, melted, cooled

FRUIT

20 to 24 whole medium strawberries, hulled

2 oz. bittersweet chocolate, melted, cooled

2 tablespoons sliced almonds

1 Heat oven to 350°F. Spray 10-inch tart pan with removable bottom with nonstick cooking spray. In food processor, combine 1 cup flour, brown sugar and salt; pulse to combine. Add 6 tablespoons butter; pulse until mixture has texture of coarse meal. In small bowl, combine 1 egg yolk and water; blend well. Add to flour mixture; pulse until dry ingredients are moistened.

2 Turn out onto work surface; press together to form dough. Press dough in bottom and up sides of tart pan.

3 Bake 20 to 25 minutes or until lightly browned. Cool on wire rack.

4 In medium saucepan, combine sugar, 2 tablespoons flour and 3 egg yolks; mix until well combined. Slowly pour milk into egg mixture, whisking constantly. Cook over medium heat, whisking constantly, until mixture thickens and comes to a boil. Remove from heat. Add 1 tablespoon butter and almond extract; stir until butter is melted. Press plastic wrap over surface of pastry cream; refrigerate 30 to 40 minutes or until cool.

5 Spread 3 oz. chocolate over cooled crust. Spread cooled pastry cream evenly over chocolate. Dip tips of strawberries into 2 oz. chocolate; place on plate. Refrigerate custard and berries until ready to serve. Place berries on tart just before serving. Garnish with sliced almonds.

8 servings

Bars, Candies & Cookies

DATE NUT COOKIES

Daphine Smith
Baytown, Texas

> 1 cup packed brown sugar
>
> 1 cup sugar plus more for dipping
>
> 1 cup shortening
>
> 3 eggs
>
> $3\frac{1}{2}$ cups all-purpose flour
>
> 2 teaspoons baking soda
>
> 1 teaspoon salt
>
> 1 teaspoon baking powder
>
> 1 tablespoon cinnamon
>
> 1 cup pecans, chopped
>
> 1 cup dates, diced

1 Heat oven to 375°F. Spray baking sheet with nonstick cooking spray. In large bowl, beat brown sugar, 1 cup sugar, shortening and eggs at medium speed until light and fluffy.

2 In medium bowl, combine flour, baking soda, salt, baking powder and cinnamon; mix well. Add flour mixture to sugar mixture; beat at low speed until combined. Fold in pecans and dates.

3 Roll dough into $1\frac{1}{2}$-inch balls. Dip bottom of glass in bowl of sugar; press balls with glass until $\frac{1}{4}$ inch thick, redipping glass in sugar before pressing each ball. Bake 9 to 12 minutes or until lightly browned.

About 5 dozen cookies

CRANBERRY-ALMOND BISCOTTI

Carol Stephan
Forest Park, Illinois

> $2\frac{1}{2}$ cups all-purpose flour
>
> $1\frac{1}{2}$ cups sugar
>
> 1 teaspoon baking powder
>
> $\frac{1}{2}$ teaspoon salt
>
> 1 teaspoon cinnamon
>
> $\frac{1}{2}$ teaspoon nutmeg
>
> $\frac{1}{2}$ cup unsalted butter, softened
>
> 2 eggs
>
> 1 teaspoon almond extract
>
> 1 (6-oz.) pkg. dried cranberries
>
> $\frac{3}{4}$ cup sliced almonds
>
> 1 egg white

1 Heat oven to 325°F. Line baking sheet with parchment paper. In medium bowl, combine flour, sugar, baking powder, salt, cinnamon and nutmeg; mix well.

2 In another medium bowl, beat butter at medium speed until soft and smooth. Add eggs and almond extract; beat well. Add to flour mixture; mix well. Stir in cranberries and almonds.

3 In small bowl, whisk egg white until foamy. Divide dough in half. Roll 1 half on large sheet of plastic wrap; shape into $14x1\frac{1}{2}$-inch log. Remove plastic wrap and place on baking sheet; repeat with remaining half of dough, arranging logs as far apart as possible on baking sheet. Press down logs to flatten slightly. Brush logs with egg white.

4 Bake 30 minutes; cool. Remove from parchment. With serrated knife, cut loaves diagonally into $\frac{1}{2}$-inch-thick slices. Reduce oven temperature to 300°F. Return to unlined baking sheet. Bake an additional 20 minutes. Cool on wire racks.

40 cookies

COLLEGE BOY'S CHERRY-TOFFEE COOKIES

Kathy Hazen
Vacaville, California

1¾ cup all-purpose flour

1 teaspoon baking soda

1 cup unsalted butter, softened

¾ cup packed brown sugar

¾ cup sugar

1 egg

1 teaspoon vanilla

2 cups old-fashioned rolled oats

2 cups dried cherries

1 cup toffee bits

1 In large bowl, sift together flour and baking soda. In another large bowl, beat butter, brown sugar and sugar at medium-high speed until light and fluffy, scraping bowl occasionally. Add egg; beat at high speed until combined. Stir in vanilla. Scrape down bowl.

2 Slowly add flour mixture to sugar mixture, beating until well blended. Stir in oats, cherries and toffee bits. Refrigerate dough 2 to 3 hours.

3 Heat oven to 350°F. Line baking sheets with parchment paper. Place large teaspoonfuls of dough 2 inches apart on baking sheets. Bake 13 to 15 minutes or until cookies are brown and crisp. Cool on baking sheets 5 minutes; finish cooling on wire racks. Store in airtight container.

5 dozen cookies

MOCHA TRUFFLES

Cecelia Rooney
Point Pleasant, New Jersey

⅓ cup heavy whipping cream

¼ cup unsalted butter, cubed

1 tablespoon instant espresso powder

½ cup white chocolate chips

2 cups semisweet chocolate chips

COATING

½ cup white chocolate chips

36 coffee beans

Unsweetened cocoa

Powdered sugar

1 In medium saucepan, heat cream and butter over medium heat. Whisk in espresso powder until completely dissolved. Reduce heat to low. Add ½ cup vanilla chips and chocolate chips; stir until melted and smooth.

2 Pour into 9-inch pie pan. Refrigerate 2 hours or until consistency is soft.

3 Line baking sheet with parchment paper. Scoop mixture with teaspoon; roll into ¾-inch balls. Place on baking sheet; refrigerate 1 hour.

4 To decorate balls, melt ½ cup vanilla chips in dry microwave-safe container in microwave on medium 30 seconds; stir. Repeat until chips are melted. Pour into resealable plastic bag. Cut bottom corner of bag; drizzle chocolate over balls. Top each ball with 1 coffee bean. Refrigerate until balls are set. When set, roll balls in cocoa or powdered sugar. Place in paper candy cups.

3 dozen truffles

LEMON RASPBERRY BARS

LEMON RASPBERRY BARS

Gloria Kniaz
Garland, Texas

CRUST

1½ cups all-purpose flour

¼ cup sugar

¼ teaspoon salt

½ cup unsalted butter, chilled, cut up

2 to 3 tablespoons water

FILLING

4 eggs

1 cup sugar

¼ cup all-purpose flour

½ teaspoon baking powder

2 teaspoons grated lemon peel

6 tablespoons fresh lemon juice

1 cup raspberry jam

Powdered sugar

1 Heat oven to 350°F. Spray 13x9-inch pan with nonstick cooking spray. In medium bowl, combine 1½ cups flour, ¼ cup sugar and salt; mix well.

2 With pastry blender or two knives, cut in butter until mixture crumbles. Add 2 tablespoons water; toss to moisten. Mixture should be moist and crumbly; if mixture seems dry, add additional water. Press mixture evenly over bottom of pan. Bake 18 to 20 minutes or until lightly browned.

3 In medium bowl, whisk together eggs, 1 cup sugar, ¼ cup flour and baking powder until well blended. Add lemon peel and lemon juice; blend well.

4 Spread raspberry jam over partially baked crust. Top with lemon mixture. Return to oven; bake an additional 20 to 25 minutes or until set and lightly browned. Cool on wire rack.

5 When cool, cut into bars; sprinkle with powdered sugar.

30 bars

SHAR'S RHUBARB COOKIES

Shar Stanton
Bowling Green, Ohio

½ cup butter-flavored shortening

1½ cups sugar

2 tablespoons milk

2 eggs

1 cup diced rhubarb

3 cups all-purpose flour

1 teaspoon baking soda

1 teaspoon cinnamon

½ teaspoon nutmeg

1 Heat oven to 350°F. Line baking sheet with parchment paper. In large bowl, beat shortening and sugar at medium speed until soft and smooth. Add milk; mix well. Add eggs one at a time, beating well after each addition. Add rhubarb; mix well.

2 In medium bowl, combine flour, baking soda, cinnamon and nutmeg; mix well.

3 Slowly add flour mixture to butter mixture, beating until well blended. Drop dough by tablespoonfuls onto baking sheet.*

4 Bake 12 to 15 minutes or until light golden brown; cool on wire rack.

TIP *For thinner cookies, flatten cookies with glass before baking.

3 dozen cookies

CARAMEL BARS

Rosemary Siewert
Apple Valley, Minnesota

1 1/2 cups all-purpose flour

1 1/2 cups old-fashioned rolled oats

1 1/4 cups packed brown sugar

3/4 teaspoon baking soda

1/4 teaspoon salt

1 cup plus 2 tablespoons butter, melted

1 (14-oz.) bag caramels

1/2 cup whipping cream

1 1/2 cups semisweet chocolate chips

1 Heat oven to 350°F. In medium bowl, combine flour, oats, brown sugar, baking soda, salt and butter; mix well. Reserve 2/3 cup; set aside. Press remaining batter in bottom of 13x9-inch pan. Bake 10 minutes. Remove from oven.

2 Meanwhile, in top of double boiler, melt caramels and cream until smooth.

3 Sprinkle baked crust with chocolate chips. Pour melted caramel mixture over chips. Sprinkle with reserved 2/3 cup crust crumbs. Bake 15 to 20 minutes or until almost firm. (Bars will be slightly soft in middle when removed from oven, but will set as they cool.)

28 bars

PUMPKIN COOKIES

Sarah Sally Bryga
Mt. Pleasant, Pennsylvania

COOKIES

1 cup butter

1 cup sugar

1/2 cup packed brown sugar

1 egg

1 cup cooked or canned pumpkin

1 teaspoon vanilla

2 cups all-purpose flour

1 teaspoon baking powder

1 teaspoon baking soda

1 teaspoon cinnamon

1/2 teaspoon salt

ICING

1/2 cup packed brown sugar

1/4 cup milk

3 tablespoons butter

1 cup powdered sugar

3/4 teaspoon vanilla

1 Heat oven to 375°F. Line baking sheets with parchment paper. In large bowl, beat 1 cup butter, sugar, 1/2 cup brown sugar and egg at medium speed until soft and smooth. Add pumpkin and 1 teaspoon vanilla; mix well.

2 In medium bowl, combine flour, baking powder, baking soda, cinnamon and salt; mix well.

3 Slowly add flour mixture to pumpkin mixture, beating until well blended. Drop by teaspoonfuls onto baking sheet. Bake 10 to 12 minutes or until cookies are light brown. Cool on wire rack.

4 To make icing, in small saucepan, combine 1/2 cup brown sugar, milk and 3 tablespoons butter; bring to a boil over medium-low heat. Stir in powdered sugar and 3/4 teaspoon vanilla. Spread icing on cooled cookies while icing is still hot.

3 1/2 dozen cookies

KAHLUA-CHOCOLATE CHIP COOKIES

Nicole Martincic
Redford, Michigan

2¼ cups all-purpose flour

1 teaspoon baking soda

1 teaspoon salt

¾ cup sugar

¾ cup packed brown sugar

¾ cup butter-flavored shortening

2 eggs

¼ cup coffee-flavored liqueur

1 teaspoon vanilla

1 (12-oz.) pkg. semisweet chocolate chips

½ cup pecans

1 Heat oven to 375°F. Line baking sheet with parchment paper. In small bowl, combine flour, baking soda and salt; mix well.

2 In large bowl, combine sugar, brown sugar and shortening; mix well. Add eggs, liqueur and vanilla; mix well. Slowly stir in flour mixture until of uniform consistency. Stir in chocolate chips and pecans. Drop onto baking sheet in teaspoonfuls 3 inches apart. Bake 10 to 11 minutes or until light brown.

About 3½ dozen cookies

PARADISE TRUFFLES

Stephanie Zonis
Neshanic Station, New Jersey

TRUFFLES

¼ cup cream of coconut

¼ cup whipping cream

¼ cup unsalted butter, cut into thin pieces

2 teaspoons grated lime peel

2 teaspoons fresh lime juice

12 oz. white chocolate, finely chopped

COATING

¾ cup powdered sugar or flaked coconut

1 In medium saucepan, combine cream of coconut, whipping cream, butter and lime peel. Heat over low heat until butter melts and mixture comes to a simmer, stirring frequently. Remove from heat. Cover; let stand 15 minutes.

2 Strain cream mixture into medium bowl. Return strained mixture to saucepan; stir in lime juice. Add chocolate; heat over very low heat, stirring constantly, until chocolate is almost all melted. Remove from heat; continue to stir until chocolate is fully melted. Pour mixture into medium bowl. Cover; refrigerate 6 to 8 hours or until mixture is firm.

3 Scoop mixture with teaspoon; roll into balls, about 1 inch in diameter. Roll balls in powdered sugar or coconut. Place in paper candy cups. Garnish with crystallized violets or lime peel, if desired.

3 dozen truffles

PETITES DOUCES AUX NOIX ET PRUNEAUX

Norman Martìnez
Miami, Florida

Cornstarch

2 cups Maria cookie crumbs*

1/2 cup chopped walnuts

1/2 cup dried prunes

1 cup condensed milk

1/2 teaspoon fresh lemon juice

1 Cut out 15-inch piece of parchment paper; dust lightly with cornstarch.

2 In medium bowl, combine cookie crumbs, walnuts, prunes, milk and lemon juice; mix until well combined. (If too dry, add additional condensed milk until mixture is soft.) Roll mixture into a ball; let rest 10 minutes.

3 Roll mixture into 3/4-inch-thick roll. Wrap in parchment paper, then in aluminum foil. Refrigerate at least 4 hours. Cut into 36 (1/4-inch-thick) rounds.

TIP * Maria cookies can be found in the Hispanic section of many grocery stores. Shortbread-style cookies can be substituted.

36 petites douces

MOM'S RUGALACH

Marlene Sinyard
Brunswick, Maine

1 cup unsalted butter, softened

1 (8-oz.) pkg. cream cheese, softened

2 cups all-purpose flour

1/3 cup sugar

1 tablespoon cinnamon

1/2 cup chopped walnuts

1/4 cup golden raisins

1/2 cup miniature semisweet chocolate chips, if desired

1 In large bowl, combine butter and cream cheese; beat at medium speed until mixture is smooth. Add flour; mix until dough forms. Divide dough into 4 pieces; shape each into flattened disk. Wrap each in plastic wrap. Refrigerate at least 2 hours or until dough is well chilled.

2 Heat oven to 375°F. Line baking sheet with parchment paper. In small bowl, combine sugar and cinnamon; mix well. Set aside.

3 On floured surface, roll one-fourth of the dough into a 12-inch round. (Keep remaining dough in refrigerator.) Sprinkle with 1/4 of sugar mixture; top with 1/4 each of the walnuts, raisins and chocolate chips. Cut into 12 wedges. Starting at wide end of each wedge, roll up; shape into crescent shape. Place on baking sheet. Repeat with remaining dough.

4 Bake 18 to 20 minutes or until browned.

4 dozen cookies

MOM'S RUGALACH

CINNAMON PECAN PETITES

Melanie Hornstein
Santa Fe, New Mexico

1 cup butter, softened

1 cup sugar

1 teaspoon vanilla

1 egg yolk

2 cups all-purpose flour

1 teaspoon cinnamon

$1/2$ cup ground pecans

1 Heat oven to 350°F. Spray 15x10x1-inch pan with nonstick cooking spray. In large bowl, beat butter and sugar at medium speed until light and fluffy. Beat in vanilla and egg yolk.

2 In medium bowl, combine flour and cinnamon. While mixing at low speed, gradually add flour mixture to butter mixture until well mixed. Spread in pan. Sprinkle pecans over top; press in.

3 Bake 20 to 25 minutes or until lightly browned. While hot, cut into 20 squares. Cut each square in half diagonally to form triangles. Cool in pan.

40 bars

APRICOT ALMOND BARS

P.J. Hamel
Hanover, New Hampshire

CRUST

1 cup all-purpose flour

$1/2$ cup butter, chilled, cut up

$1/4$ cup water

FILLING

1 cup water

$1/2$ cup butter, cut up

1 cup all-purpose flour

2 eggs, room temperature

2 teaspoons almond extract

TOPPING

$1/2$ cup apricot jam, warmed

$1/4$ cup slivered or sliced almonds, toasted

$1/2$ cup powdered sugar

2 to $2^1/2$ teaspoons milk

$1/4$ teaspoon almond extract

1 Heat oven to 350°F. Spray 13x9-inch pan with nonstick cooking spray. Place 1 cup flour in medium bowl. With pastry blender or two knives, cut in $1/2$ cup butter until it is the size of peas. Add $1/4$ cup water; mix until dough forms. Flatten dough into a disk. Press dough evenly in bottom of pan. Cover; refrigerate 30 minutes.

2 In medium saucepan over medium heat, bring 1 cup water and $1/2$ cup butter to a boil. Pour boiling mixture into large bowl. Add 1 cup flour; beat at medium speed until smooth and flour is absorbed. Add eggs one at a time, beating well after each addition. Stir in 2 teaspoons almond extract.

3 Spread batter over dough in pan, covering completely. Bake 50 to 55 minutes or until deep golden brown. Remove from oven. Spread with apricot jam; sprinkle with almonds. Cool on wire rack.

4 Meanwhile, in small bowl, combine powdered sugar, milk and $1/4$ teaspoon almond extract; mix until smooth. Drizzle over cooled bars.

36 bars

NUSSECKEN

Colleen Ann Haney
St. Paul, Minnesota

TOPPING

7 oz. hazelnuts

²⁄₃ cup sugar

7 tablespoons butter

1 teaspoon vanilla

2 tablespoons water

PASTRY

1¹⁄₃ cups all-purpose flour

6 tablespoons sugar

¹⁄₂ teaspoon baking powder

1 teaspoon vanilla

1 egg

5 tablespoons butter, cut into pieces

¹⁄₂ cup apricot jam

ICING

3 oz. bittersweet or semisweet chocolate, chopped

2 tablespoons milk

1 In food processor, pulse hazelnuts until half of nuts are ground and half are chopped. Set aside.

2 In medium saucepan, combine sugar, butter and vanilla. Cook over medium heat until butter is melted. Add water; bring to a full boil. Stir in hazelnuts. Remove from heat; cool to room temperature.

3 Heat oven to 375°F. In medium bowl, combine flour, 6 tablespoons sugar and baking powder; mix well. Make a well in center of flour mixture. Add vanilla and egg; blend with fork, incorporating some of flour mixture, until egg mixture forms a paste. Add 5 tablespoons butter; blend with pastry blender or fingers until mixture crumbles.

4 With lightly floured fingers, press dough in bottom of ungreased 15x10x1-inch pan. Spread evenly with jam. Spread cooled topping over jam.

5 Bake 20 to 25 minutes or until lightly browned. Cool. Cut into 12 pieces; cut pieces in half to form triangles.

6 Line baking sheet with parchment paper. In small saucepan, combine chocolate and milk; melt over low heat, stirring until smooth. Dip two corners of each triangle in chocolate; place on baking sheet. Cool until firm.

24 bars

CHOCOLATE CHIP-OATMEAL-WALNUT BARS

CHOCOLATE CHIP-OATMEAL-WALNUT BARS

Diane Neuneder
Milwaukee, Wisconsin

1 cup butter, softened

¾ cup packed brown sugar

½ cup sugar

2 teaspoons vanilla

2 eggs

1¼ cups old-fashioned rolled oats

1 cup whole wheat flour

¼ cup all-purpose flour

1 teaspoon baking soda

Dash salt

1 (12-oz.) pkg. chocolate chips

1½ cups chopped walnuts, toasted*

1 Heat oven to 375°F. In large bowl, beat butter at medium speed until soft and smooth. Add brown sugar, sugar and vanilla; blend well. Add eggs one at a time, beating well after each addition.

2 In medium bowl, combine oats, whole wheat flour, all-purpose flour, baking soda and salt; mix well.

3 Slowly add flour mixture to butter mixture, beating until well blended. Stir in chocolate chips and walnuts. Spoon and spread dough into ungreased 15x10x1-inch baking pan.

4 Bake 15 to 20 minutes or until golden brown; cool on wire rack.

TIP *To toast nuts, spread on baking sheet; bake at 375°F for 7 to 10 minutes or until lightly browned. Cool.

48 bars

DOUBLE DECKER FUDGE

Lori Kennison
Jacksonville, Florida

2½ cups sugar

¾ cup evaporated milk

⅓ cup unsalted butter

½ teaspoon salt

3 cups miniature marshmallows

1 (6-oz.) pkg. butterscotch chips

½ cup chopped walnuts

½ teaspoon maple extract

1 to 1½ pkg. milk chocolate chips

1 teaspoon vanilla

1 Line 8-inch square pan with aluminum foil. In large saucepan, combine sugar, milk, butter and salt. Bring to a boil over medium-high heat, stirring constantly. Boil 7 minutes, stirring constantly. Remove from heat. Stir in marshmallows; mix until smooth.

2 Place half of marshmallow mixture in medium bowl. Add butterscotch chips, walnuts and maple extract; stir until chips are melted and mixture is smooth. Set aside.

3 Add chocolate chips and vanilla to remaining marshmallow mixture; stir until chips are melted and mixture is smooth. Spread in pan. Top with butterscotch mixture. Refrigerate 2 to 3 hours or until firm. Cut into 1-inch pieces.

30 pieces

AFGHANS

Amy Smith
Mt. Shasta, California

¾ cup plus 2 tablespoons butter

½ cup sugar

1¼ cups all-purpose flour

¼ cup unsweetened cocoa

2 cups cornflakes cereal

15 walnuts, halved

GLAZE

½ cup milk chocolate chips

1 tablespoon unsalted butter

1 tablespoon light corn syrup

1 tablespoon hot water (115°F to 120°F)

1 Heat oven to 350°F. Spray 15x10x1-inch pan with nonstick cooking spray. In large bowl, beat butter and sugar until smooth and creamy. Stir in flour and cocoa; mix well. Gently fold in cereal. Drop mixture by tablespoonfuls onto baking sheet; press lightly with fork.

2 Bake 15 to 20 minutes or until lightly browned around edges. Cool on wire rack.

3 To make glaze, in small saucepan over low heat, melt chocolate and butter; stir in corn syrup and water. Drizzle over cooled cookies; decorate each cookie with 1 walnut half.

15 cookies

GATEAUX BONBONS

Carol Jackson
Broken Arrow, Oklahoma

⅔ cup butter, softened

1 cup sugar

1 egg

1 (3-oz.) pkg. cream cheese, softened

½ teaspoon fresh lemon juice

1 teaspoon grated lemon peel

2 cups all-purpose flour

½ teaspoon baking powder

½ teaspoon salt

¼ cup orange marmalade

1 In large bowl, beat butter, sugar, egg, cream cheese, lemon juice and lemon peel until light and fluffy. In medium bowl, combine flour, baking powder and salt; mix well. Add to butter mixture; mix well. Refrigerate 1 hour.

2 Heat oven to 350°F. Spray 15x10x1-inch baking pan with nonstick cooking spray. Divide dough into 4 portions. Keeping remaining dough refrigerated, on lightly floured surface, roll 1 portion to ⅛-inch thickness. Cut into 1-inch rounds. Spread with floured hands to form 1-inch circle. Repeat with remaining dough portions.

3 Place half of rounds on baking sheet. Spread each with ¼ teaspoon marmalade. Cover with remaining rounds. With floured fingers, seal edges. Bake 8 to 10 minutes or until edges are light brown. Cool on wire rack.

32 cookies

GRANDMA'S SOFT WHITE COOKIES

Cyndy Larson
Minneapolis, Minnesota

4$\frac{1}{2}$ cups all-purpose flour

2 cups sugar

1 cup sour cream

1 cup shortening

3 eggs

1 teaspoon baking soda

$\frac{1}{2}$ teaspoon salt

1 teaspoon vanilla

1 In large bowl, combine flour, sugar, sour cream, shortening, eggs, baking soda, salt and vanilla; mix well. Cover. Refrigerate overnight.

2 Heat oven to 350°F. Roll dough into balls; flatten. Place on baking sheets; bake 10 to 12 minutes. Cool on wire rack.

4$\frac{1}{2}$ dozen cookies

MOIST CHERRY CAKE

Donna Nofzinger
Port Charlotte, Florida

1 tablespoon unsalted butter, softened

1$\frac{1}{2}$ cups sugar

1 cup all-purpose flour

1 teaspoon baking soda

1 teaspoon cinnamon

1 egg, beaten

$\frac{1}{2}$ cup chopped walnuts

$\frac{1}{2}$ cup chopped pecans

1 (14.5-oz.) can sour cherries, drained, juice reserved

2 teaspoons cornstarch

Dash salt

Whipped cream

1 Heat oven to 350°F. Lightly grease 8-inch square pan. In large bowl, combine butter, 1 cup of the sugar, flour, baking soda, cinnamon, egg, walnuts, pecans and cherries; mix well. Pour into pan; bake 40 to 45 minutes or until toothpick inserted near center comes out clean. Cool.

2 In medium saucepan, combine remaining $\frac{1}{2}$ cup sugar, cornstarch, salt and reserved cherry juice. Heat over medium-high heat until thickened.

3 Pour sauce over cake; let sit 5 minutes. Cut into squares. Serve with cream.

12 servings

PEANUT BUTTER-WALNUT COOKIES

Isaiah Clark III
Roanoke Rapids, North Carolina

1 cup butter

1 cup packed brown sugar

1 cup sugar

1 cup crunchy peanut butter

2 eggs

2½ cups all-purpose flour

½ teaspoon baking soda

½ teaspoon salt

½ cup crushed walnuts

1 Heat oven to 375°F. Line baking sheets with parchment paper. In large bowl, beat butter at medium speed until soft and smooth. Add brown sugar, sugar and peanut butter; blend well. Add eggs one at a time, beating well after each addition.

2 In medium bowl, combine flour, baking soda and salt; mix well.

3 Slowly add flour mixture to butter mixture, beating until well blended. Stir in walnuts. Drop dough by teaspoonfuls onto baking sheets. Flatten each mound of dough with fork. Bake 10 to 12 minutes or until golden brown. Cool on wire rack.

About 3 dozen cookies

WHITE CHOCOLATE-MACADAMIA NUT COOKIES

Cecelia Rooney
Point Pleasant, New Jersey

1 cup all-purpose flour

¼ teaspoon baking powder

⅛ teaspoon salt

⅛ teaspoon baking soda

1 teaspoon vanilla

1 egg

½ cup plus 2 tablespoons butter

¼ cup packed brown sugar

1½ cups white chocolate chips

½ cup coarsely chopped macadamia nuts

1 Heat oven to 375°F. Line baking sheets with parchment paper.

2 In large bowl, combine flour, baking powder, salt and baking soda; mix well. Beat in vanilla and egg. Add butter and brown sugar; mix well. Stir in chocolate chips and nuts. Drop by teaspoonfuls 2 inches apart onto baking sheets.

3 Bake 10 minutes or until lightly browned. Cool on baking sheets 3 minutes. Finish cooling on wire racks.

3 dozen cookies

WHITE CHOCOLATE-MACADAMIA NUT COOKIES

ROCKS

Cyndy Larson
Minneapolis, Minnesota

2$\frac{1}{2}$ cups all-purpose flour

1 cup packed brown sugar

3 eggs, beaten

$\frac{2}{3}$ cup butter-flavored shortening

2 tablespoons molasses

Dash salt

1 cup raisins

1 cup chopped nuts

1 teaspoon baking soda

1 teaspoon vanilla

1 Heat oven to 350°F. Spray 15x10x1-inch pan with nonstick cooking spray.

2 In large bowl, combine flour, sugar, eggs, shortening, molasses, salt, raisins, nuts, baking soda and vanilla; mix well. Drop by spoonfuls onto baking sheet. Bake 12 to 15 minutes or until lightly browned. Cool on wire rack.

3 $\frac{1}{2}$ dozen cookies

CARAMEL BROWNIES

Jeff and Abby Wilson
Minneapolis, Minnesota

1 package German chocolate cake mix

$\frac{3}{4}$ cup butter, melted

$\frac{2}{3}$ cup evaporated milk

14 oz. caramels

1 (6- oz.) pkg. semisweet chocolate chips

1 Heat oven to 350°F. Spray 13x9-inch pan with nonstick cooking spray; lightly flour.

2 In large bowl, combine cake mix, butter and $\frac{1}{3}$ cup of the milk; press half of mixture into pan.

3 In medium saucepan, combine caramels and remaining $\frac{1}{3}$ cup milk. Cook over medium heat until caramels are melted, stirring occasionally. Pour over cake batter in pan; sprinkle with chocolate chips. Top with reserved cake batter. Bake 15 to 20 minutes, cool.

30 brownies

Index

RECIPE INDEX

Afghans, 148

Almond Cheesecake, 129

Andy's Favorite Meatballs, 78

Apple Crisp Pie, 133

Apple Tart, 132

Apricot Almond Bars, 144

Artichoke And Pork Sauté, 67

Asparagus And Shrimp Penne With
    Saffron, 97

Asparagus Salad, 32

Asparagus With Toasted Almonds And
    Garlic, 53

Autumn Baked Carrots, 53

Bacon-Cabbage Soup, 47

Baked Salmon Cakes, 98

Banana Bread, 24

Bananas Foster, 122

Beef 'N' Tater Bake, 78

Beef Carbonnade, 75

Black Bean Salsa, 11

Black Beans And Rice, 56

Blueberry Buckle, 128

Blueberry Muffins, 30

Bow Tie Pasta With Roasted
    Vegetables, 110

Buttermilk Raisin Pie, 116

Cajun Barbeque Shrimp, 97

Caramel Apple Crunch Pie, 133

Caramel Bars, 140

Caramel Brownies, 152

Caramel Rolls With Sweet Dough, 22

Carrot Soup, 39

Cassoulet With Lamb, 72

Cauliflower Curry With Potatoes And
    Peas, 110

Cheese Bread, 18

Cheese-Rice Loaf, 55

Chicken Adobo, 83

Chicken And Crab Richele, 82

Chicken Bog, 84

Chicken Confetti Salad, 45

Chicken Fiesta, 88

Chicken Formaggio Pizza, 81

Chicken Piccata, 87

Chipolte Lime Sauce, 83

Chocolate Box Cake With Strawberries
    And Cream, 116

Chocolate Chip-Oatmeal-Walnut Bars,
    147

Chocolate Chip-Pecan Bread, 23

Chocolate Chunk Banana Bread, 21

Chocolate Zucchini Bread, 23

Chocolate-Dipped Strawberry Tart, 134

Cinnamon Pecan Petites, 144

Citrus-Marinated Pork Tenderloin, 75

Cocoa Pound Cake, 128

College Boy's Cherry-Toffee Cookies,
    137

Corn Custard, 50

Cosmopolitan Bread Pudding, 130

Cousin Ada's Butterflake Rolls, 19

Crab And Shrimp Bisque, 44

Crab Cheesecake, 9

Crab-Stuffed Mushroom Caps, 7

Cranberry Zucchini Bread, 29

Cranberry-Almond Biscotti, 136

Cranberry-Port Relish, 60

Cream Biscuits, 18

Creamy Corn And Zucchini, 60

Creamy Scrambled Eggs, 105

Crisp Rosemary Potatoes, 55

Cruchy-Munchy Chicken Salad, 45

Cucumber Dip, 15

Date Nut Cookies, 136

Decadent Double-Chocolate Layer
    Cake, 127

Distant And Delicious Broiled Salmon,
    99

Double Decker Fudge, 147

Dried Fruit Bread, 29

Easy Homemade Sausage, 53

Eggplant Stuffed Peppers, 59

Eggplant-Stuffed Ravioli, 113

Eggs McGlasson, 114

English Trifle, 120

Fancy Hot Artichoke Dip, 14

French Onion Torte, 112

Fruit Pizza, 130

Fruited Tofu Curry, 108

Fruit-Nut Salad With Curry
    Vinaigrette, 41

Fudge Pie, 128

Gâteaux Bonbons, 148

German Apple Cake, 125

German-Style Roast, 76

Ginger Crab Cakes, 10

Glazed Pecans, 10

Grandma's Soft White Cookies, 149

Great Aunt Katie's Sausage Berok, 77

Greek Spinach Cheese Pie, 108

Green Chile Corn Bread, 21

Grilled Steak Salad, 66

Heavenly Corn Pudding, 59

Herbed Chicken Salad, 48

Honey-Gingered Pork Tenderloin, 71

Honey-Lime Marinated Swordfish, 99

Hoppin' John, 60

Hot Cinnamon Rolls, 26

Hot Open-Faced Zucchini Sandwiches,
    7

Hummus, 12

Individual Tiramisu Desserts, 121

Italian Garden Pasta Salad, 37

Italian Shrimp Fettucine, 102

Italian Wedding Soup, 32

Jalapeño Cheese Biscuits, 30

Jamaican Shrimp Curry, 102

Javanese Peanut Pasta, 104

Jerk Rub For Chicken, 82

Joanna's Signature Salad, 44

Kahlua-Chocolate Chip Cookies, 141

Key Lime Citrus Freeze, 11

Kimberly's Low-Fat Cranberry-Apple
    Bread, 18

Kimberly's Peach-Almond Streusel Pie,
    125

King's Kraze With Boiled Custard, 120

Lemon Pie, 117

Lemon Raspberry Bars, 139

Lemon Yogurt Cake, 119

Lemon-Blueberry Cheesecake, 121

Lemon-Poppy Seed Bread, 19

Lentil Tomato Soup, 46

Lobster Pasta Richele, 100

Mandarin Orange Nut Salad, 40

Maque Choux, 54

Marlene's Soft White Sandwich Bread,
    19

Medallions Of Veal Trocadero, 70

Melissa's Salsa, 14

Messy Chicken, 83

Mexican Casserole, 66
Minestrone, 33
Mini Quiche Cups, 12
Moist Cherry Cake, 149
Mocha Truffles, 137
Mom's Rugalach, 142
Mushroom And Sour Cream Pie, 112
Mussels In Saffron Broth, 94
Mussels In White Sauce, 95
Mustard Basting Sauce For Chicken, 88
My Favorite Bruschetta, 12
My Favorite Cabbage Salad, 42
Naples Train Station Roasted Red Peppers, 56
No-Bake Fresh Peach Pie, 124
No-Bake Mascarpone Key Lime Pie, 119
Nussecken, 145
Orange-Marinated Pork Chops, 62
Osso Buco With Gremolata, 64
Oven Chicken Cacciatore, 81
Oven-Braised Brisket With Onions, 69
Paradise Truffles, 141
Parmesan Cheese And Herb Crostini, 6
Party Ham Rolls, 15
Pasta And Sausage Soup, 42
Pasta Portobello, 109
Pasta With Swiss Chard And Smoked Gouda, 114
Peanut Butter Walnut Cookies, 150
Penne With Vodka, 107
Pepper And Potato Omelet, 104
Pierogies, 51
Pesto Chicken Salad, 36
Pesto Toasts, 16
Petites Douces Aux Noix Et Pruneaux, 142
Pheasant With Pomegranate Sauce, 62
Pizza Rustica, 95
Poached Scallops With Curry, 91
Pomodoro Sauce For Pasta, 109
Pork Medallions With Green Peppercorn Sauce, 69
Pork With Green Olives And Tomatoes, 76

Potato Balls, 11
Pumpkin Cookies, 140
Pumpkin-Banana Muffins, 24
Ralph's Waffles, 105
Red Beet Chocolate Cake, 117
Red Potato Salad With Chardonnay Vinaigrette, 47
Rhubarb Bread, 27
Rigatoni Carbonara, 67
Risotto, 51
Roasted Red Pepper & Garlic Spread, 15
Rocks, 152
Romaine And Cucumber Salad With Garlic Vinaigrette, 44
Rosemary Chicken In Artichoke Sauce, 88
Saffron-Scented Chowder, 41
Salad With Avocado Dressing, 36
Santa Fe Seafood Stew, 100
Scalloped Tomatoes, 50
Seafood Gumbo, 90
Sesame Shrimp Soba Salad, 34
Shar's Rhubarb Cookies, 139
Shrimp Scampi, 99
Shrimp Sicilian, 91
Shrimp With Tasso Gravy, 92
Simple Salad In Jicama Bowl, 37
Skillet Cabbage, 50
Smoked Sausage And New Potatoes, 74
Sour Cream Carrot Cake, 124
Southern Candied Sweet Potatoes, 54
South-Of-The-Border Casserole With Bell Peppers And Onions, 72
Spanish Rice, 54
Spicy Shrimp William, 92
Spinach Fettuccine With Scallops, 90
Spinach Frittata, 109
Spinach Soup With Cheese Foam, 40
Squash And Roasted Corn Chowder, 39
Squash And Walnut Pie, 122
Steak L'Macha, 63
Strawberry & Spinach Salad With Poppy Seed Dressing, 48
Summer Melon Smoothie, 6
Summertime Sun Punch, 12

Sunday Chicken With Sausage And Polenta, 84
Sun-Dried Tomato Dip, 10
Sweet-Tart Ribs, 63
Tangerine Tango, 11
Texas Caviar Salad, 40
Texas Pecan Pie, 122
Thick Pork Chops On The Grill, 74
Three Cheese Tortellini, 114
Tofu And Broccoli Pie, 105
Tomatillo Salsa, 16
Tri-Color Vegetable Couscous Salad, 46
Tropical Lime Bread, 27
Tuna Fiorintino, 94
Tuna Salad, 33
Turkey Bundles With Spinach, 87
Veal Scaloppini, 71
Vegetable Lasagna, 107
Warm Cannellini Bean Salad, 32
White Chocolate Macadamia Nut Cookies, 150
Wonton Cups, 6
Zucchini Soup, 33
Zucchini Squares, 14

GENERAL INDEX

A

Afghans, 148
Almonds
    Apricot, Bars, 144
    Asparagus With Toasted, And
        Garlic, 53
    Cheesecake, 129
    Cranberry-, Biscotti, 136
    Kimberly's Peach, Streusel Pie, 125
Andy's Favorite Meatballs, 78
Appetizers
    Black Bean Salsa, 11
    Crab Cheesecake, 9
    Crab-Stuffed Mushroom Caps, 7
    Cucumber Dip, 15
    Fancy Hot Artichoke Dip, 14
    Ginger Crab Cakes, 10
    Glazed Pecans, 10
    Hummus, 12
    Mini Quiche Cups, 12
    My Favorite Bruschetta, 12
    Parmesan Cheese And Herb
        Crostini, 6
    Party Ham Rolls, 15
    Pesto Toasts, 16
    Potato Balls, 11
    Roasted Red Pepper & Garlic
        Spread, 15
    Sun-Dried Tomato Dip, 10
    Tomatillo Salsa, 16
    Wonton Cups, 6
    Zucchini Squares, 14
Apples
    Caramel, Crunch Pie, 133
    Crisp Pie, 133
    German, Cake, 125
    Kimberly's Low-Fat Cranberry-
        Bread, 18
    Tart, 132
Apricot Almond Bars, 144
Artichokes
    Fancy Hot, Dip, 14
    And Pork Sauté, 67
    Rosemary Chicken In, Sauce, 88
Asparagus
    Salad, 32
    And Shrimp Penne With Saffron,
        97
    With Toasted Almonds And Garlic,
        53
Autumn Baked Carrots, 53
Avocado, Salad With, Dressing, 36

B

Bacon-Cabbage Soup, 47
Baked Salmon Cakes, 98
Banana(s)
    Bread, 24
    Chocolate Chunk, Bread, 21
    Foster, 122
    Pumpkin- Muffins, 24
Bars, Candies, & Cookies
    Afghans, 148
    Apricot Almond Bars, 144
    Caramel Bars, 140
    Caramel Brownies, 152
    Chocolate Chip-Oatmeal-Walnut
        Bars, 147
    Cinnamon Pecan Petits, 144
    College Boy's Cherry-Toffee
        Cookies, 137
    Cranberry-Almond Biscotti, 136
    Date Nut Cookies, 136
    Double Decker Fudge, 147
    Gâteaux Bonbons, 148
    Grandma's Soft White Cookies, 149
    Kahlua-Chocolate Chip Cookies,
        141
    Lemon Raspberry Bars, 139
    Mocha Truffles, 137
    Mom's Rugalach, 142
    Nussecken, 145
    Paradise Truffles, 141
    Peanut Butter-Walnut Cookies, 150
    Petits Douces Aux Noix Et
        Pruneaux, 142
    Pumpkin Cookies, 140
    Rocks, 152
    Shar's Rhubarb Cookies, 139
    White Chocolate-Macadamia Nut
        Cookies, 150
Beans
    Black, Salsa, 11
    Black, And Rice, 56
    Hoppin' John, 60
    Hummus, 12
    South-Of-The-Border Casserole, 72
    Warm Cannellini, Salad, 32
Beef
    Carbonnade, 75
    German-Style Roast, 76
    Grilled Steak Salad, 66
    'N' Tater Bake, 78
    Oven-Braised Brisket With Onions,
        69
    Steak L'Macha, 63

Beverages
    Key Lime Citrus Freeze, 11
    Summer Melon Smoothie, 6
    Summertime Sun Punch, 12
    Tangerine Tango, 11
Biscuits
    Cream, 18
    Jalapeño Cheese, 30
Black Bean Salsa, 11
Black Beans And Rice, 56
Blueberries
    Buckle, 128
    Lemon-, Cheesecake, 121
    Muffins, 30
Bow Tie Pasta With Roasted
    Vegetables, 110
Bread Pudding, Cosmopolitan, 130
Breads
    Banana, 24
    Blueberry Muffins, 30
    Caramel Rolls With Sweet Dough,
        22
    Cheese, 18
    Chocolate Chip-Pecan, 23
    Chocolate Chunk Banana, 21
    Chocolate Zucchini, 23
    Cousin Ada's Butterflake Rolls, 19
    Cranberry Zucchini, 29
    Cream Biscuits, 18
    Dried Fruit, 29
    Green Chile Corn, 21
    Hot Cinnamon Rolls, 26
    Jalapeño Cheese Biscuits, 30
    Kimberly's Low-Fat Cranberry-
        Apple, 18
    Lemon-Poppy Seed, 19
    Marlene's Soft White Sandwich, For
        Bread Machines, 19
    Pumpklin-Banana Muffins, 24
    Rhubarb, 27
    Tropical Lime, 27
Broccoli
    Chicken Confetti Salad, 45
    Sesame Shrimp Soba Salad, 34
    Tofu And, Pie, 105
Buttermilk Raisin Pie, 116

C

Cabbage
    Bacon-, Soup, 47
    My Favorite, Salad, 42
    Skillet, 50
Cajun Barbecue Shrimp, 97

Cakes. See Under Desserts
Candies. See Bars, Candies, & Cookies
Caramel
　　Apple Crunch Pie, 133
　　Bars, 140
　　Brownies, 152
　　Rolls With Sweet Dough, 22
Carrots
　　Autumn Baked, 53
　　Soup, 39
　　Sour Cream, Cake, 124
Casserole(s)
　　Beef 'N' Tater Bake, 78
　　Mexican, 66
　　Smoked Sausage And New Potatoes
　　　　With Bell Peppers And Onions,
　　　　74
　　South-Of-The-Border, 72
Cassoulet With Lamb, 72
Cauliflower
　　Chicken Confetti Salad, 45
　　Curry With Potatoes And Peas, 110
Cheese
　　Bread, 18
　　Crab Cheesecake, 9
　　Greek Spinach-, Pie, 108
　　Jalapeño, Biscuits, 30
　　Mini Quiche Cups, 12
　　Parmesan, And Herb Crostini, 6
　　Pasta With Swiss Chard And
　　　　Smoked Gouda, 114
　　-Rice Loaf, 55
　　Three, Tortellini, 114
　　Wonton Cups, 6
Cherries
　　College Boy's, -Toffee Cookies, 137
Chicken
　　Adobo, 83
　　Bog, 84
　　Confetti Salad, 45
　　And Crab Richele, 82
　　Crunchy-Munchy, Salad, 45
　　Fiesta, 88
　　Formaggio Pizza, 81
　　Herbed, Salad, 48
　　Jerk Rub For, 82
　　Messy, 83
　　Mustard Basting Sauce For, 88
　　Oven, Cacciatore, 81
　　Pesto, Salad, 36
　　Piccata, 87
　　Rosemary, In Artichoke Sauce, 88
　　Sunday, With Sausage And Polenta, 84

Chipotle Lime Sauce, 83
Chocolate
　　Box Cake With Strawberries And
　　　　Cream, 116
　　Caramel Brownies, 152
　　Chip-Oatmeal-Walnut Bars, 147
　　Chip -Pecan Bread, 23
　　Chunk Banana Bread, 21
　　Decadent Double-, Layer Cake, 127
　　-Dipped Strawberry Tart, 134
　　Double Decker Fudge, 147
　　Kahlua-, Chip Cookies, 141
　　Red Beet, Cake, 117
　　White, -Macadamia Nut Cookies,
　　　　150
　　Zucchini Bread, 23
Cinnamon Pecan Petits, 144
Citrus-Marinated Pork Tenderloin, 75
Cocoa Pound Cake, 128
College Boy's Cherry-Toffee Cookies, 137
**Cookies. See Bars, Candies, &
Cookies**
Corn
　　Creamy, And Zucchini, 60
　　Custard, 50
　　Green Chile Bread, 21
　　Heavenly, Pudding, 59
　　Maque Choux, 54
　　Squash And Roasted, Chowder, 39
Cosmopolitan Bread Pudding, 130
Couscous, Tri-Color Vegetable, Salad, 46
Cousin Ada's Butterflake Rolls, 19
Crab
　　Cheesecake, 9
　　Chicken And, Richele, 82
　　Ginger, Cakes, 10
　　And Shrimp Bisque, 44
　　-Stuffed Mushroom Caps, 7
Cranberries
　　-Almond Biscotti, 136
　　Kimberly's Low-Fat -Apple Bread, 18
　　Port Relish, 60
　　-Zucchini Bread, 29
Cream Biscuits, 18
Creamy Corn And Zucchini, 60
Creamy Scrambled Eggs, 105
Crisp Rosemary Potatoes, 55
Crunchy-Munchy Chicken Salad, 45
Cucumber
　　Dip, 15
　　Romaine And, Salad With Garlic
　　　　Vinaigrette, 44
Curry

　　Cauliflower, With Potatoes And Peas,
　　　　110
　　Fruit-Nut Salad With, Vinaigrette, 41
　　Fruited Tofu, 108
　　Jamaican Shrimp, 102
　　Poached Scallops With, 91

D
Date Nut Cookies, 136
Decadent Double-Chocolate Layer
　　Cake, 127
Desserts
　　Almond Cheesecake, 129
　　Apple Crisp Pie, 133
　　Apple Tart, 132
　　Bananas Foster, 122
　　Blueberry Buckle, 128
　　Buttermilk Raisin Pie, 116
　　Caramel Apple Crunch Pie, 133
　　Chocolate Box Cake With
　　　　Strawberries And Cream, 116
　　Chocolate-Dipped Strawberry Tart,
　　　　134
　　Cocoa Pound Cake, 128
　　Cosmopolitan Bread Pudding, 130
　　Decadent Double-Chocolate Layer
　　　　Cake, 127
　　English Trifle, 120
　　Fruit Pizza, 130
　　Fudge Pie, 128
　　German Apple Cake, 125
　　Individual Tiramisu Desserts, 121
　　Kimberly's Peach-Almond Streusel
　　　　Pie, 125
　　King's Kraze With Boiled Custard,
　　　　120
　　Lemon-Blueberry Cheesecake, 121
　　Lemon Pie, 117
　　Lemon Yogurt Cake, 119
　　Moist Cherry Cake, 149
　　No-Bake Fresh Peach Pie, 124
　　No-Bake Mascarpone Key Lime Pie,
　　　　119
　　Red Beet Chocolate Cake, 117
　　Sour Cream Carrot Cake, 124
　　Squash And Walnut Pie, 122
　　Texas Pecan Pie, 122
Distant And Delicious Broiled Salmon,
　　99
Double Decker Fudge, 147
Dried Fruit Bread, 29

E

Easy Homemade Sausage, 53

Eggplant

    Bow Tie Pasta With Roasted
        Vegetables, 110

    -Stuffed Peppers, 59

    -Stuffed Ravioli, 113

Eggs

    Creamy Scrambled, 105

    McGlasson, 114

    Mini Quiche Cups, 12

    Pepper And Potato Omelet, 104

    Spinach Frittata, 109

English Trifle, 120

F

Fancy Hot Artichoke Dip, 14

Fish And Seafood

    Asparagus And Shrimp Penne With
        Saffron, 97

    Baked Salmon Cakes, 98

    Cajun Barbecue Shrimp, 97

    Distant And Delicious Broiled
        Salmon, 99

    Honey-Lime Marinated Swordfish,
        99

    Lobster Pasta Richele, 100

    Mussels In Saffron Broth, 94

    Mussels In White Wine, 95

    Pizza Rustica, 95

    Poached Scallops With Curry, 91

    Santa Fe Seafood Stew, 100

    Seafood Gumbo, 90

    Shrimp Scampi, 99

    Shrimp Sicilian, 91

    Shrimp With Tasso Gravy, 92

    Spicy Shrimp William, 92

    Spinach Fettuccine With Scallops,
        90

    Tuna Fiorintino, 94

French Onion Torte, 112

Fruit Pizza, 130

Fruited Tofu Curry, 108

Fruit-Nut Salad With Curry
    Vinaigrette, 41

Fudge Pie, 128

G

Gâteaux Bonbons, 148

German Apple Cake, 125

German-Style Roast, 76

Ginger Crab Cakes, 10

Glazed Pecans, 10

Grandma's Soft White Cookies, 149

Great Aunt Katie's Sausage Berok, 77

Greek Spinach-Cheese Pie, 108

Green Chile Corn Bread, 21

Gremolata, Osso Buco With, 64

Grilled Steak Salad, 66

Ground Beef

    Andy's Favorite Meatballs, 78

    Mexican Casserole, 66

    South-Of-The-Border Casserole, 72

H

Ham

    Party, Rolls, 15

    Rigatoni Carbonara, 67

Heavenly Corn Pudding, 59

Herbed Chicken Salad, 48

Honey-Gingered Pork Tenderloin, 71

Honey-Lime Marinated Swordfish, 99

Hoppin' John, 60

Hot Cinnamon Rolls, 26

Hot Open-Faced Zucchini Sandwiches, 7

Hummus, 12

I

Individual Tiramisu Desserts, 121

Italian Garden Pasta Salad, 37

Italian Shrimp Fettuccine, 102

Italian Wedding Soup, 32

J

Jalapeño Cheese Biscuits, 30

Jamaican Shrimp Curry, 102

Javanese Peanut Pasta, 104

Jerk Rub For Chicken, 82

Jicama, Simple Salad In, Bowl, 37

Joanna's Signature Salad, 44

K

Kahlua-Chocolate Chip Cookies, 141

Key Lime

    Citrus Freeze, 11

    No-Bake Mascarpone, Pie, 119

Kimberly's Low-Fat Cranberry-Apple,
    18

Kimberly's Peach-Almond Streusel Pie,
    125

King's Kraze With Boiled Custard, 120

L

Lamb, Cassoulet With, 72

Lasagna, Vegetable, 107

Lemon

    -Blueberry Cheesecake, 121

    Pie, 117

-Poppy Seed Bread, 19

Raspberry Bars, 139

Yogurt Cake, 119

Lentil Tomato Soup, 46

Lime. See Also Key Lime

    Chipolte, Sauce, 83

    Tropical, Bread, 27

Lobster Pasta Richele, 100

M

Macadamia, White Chocolate,
    Cookies, 150

Maque Choux, 54

Main Dish Pies

    French Onion Torte, 112

    Greek Spinach-Cheese Pie, 108

    Mushroom And Sour Cream Pie,
        112

    Tofu And Broccoli Pie, 105

Mandarin Orange Nut Salad, 40

Marlene's Soft White Sandwich, Bread,
    19

Meatballs, Andy's Favorite, 78

Medallions Of Veal Trocadero, 70

Melissa's Salsa, 14

Melon, Summer, Smoothie, 6

Messy Chicken, 83

Mexican Casserole, 66

Minestrone Soup, 33

Mini Quiche Cups, 12

Mocha Truffles, 137

Moist Cherry Cake, 149

Mom's Rugalach, 142

Mushroom(s)

    Chicken Fiesta, 88

    Crab-Stuffed, Caps, 7

    Pasta Portobello, 109

    And Sour Cream Pie, 112

    Steak L'Macha, 63

Mussels

    In Saffron Broth, 94

    In White Wine, 95

Mustard Basting Sauce For Chicken,
    88

My Favorite Bruschetta, 12

My Favorite Cabbage Salad, 42

N

Naples Train Station Roasted Red
    Peppers, 56

No-Bake Fresh Peach Pie, 124

No-Bake Mascarpone Key Lime Pie, 119

Nussecken, 145

O

Oatmeal, Chocolate Chip-, -Walnut Bars, 147
Olives, Pork With Green, And Tomatoes, 76

Onions
  French, Torte, 112
  Oven-Braised Brisket With, 69
  Smoked Sausage And New Potatoes With Bell Peppers And, 74
Orange-Marinated Pork Chops, 62
Osso Buco With Gremolata, 64
Oven-Braised Brisket With Onions, 69
Oven Chicken Cacciatore, 81

P

Paradise Truffles, 141
Parmesan Cheese And Herb Crostini, 6
Party Ham Rolls, 15

Pasta
  Bow Tie, With Roasted Vegetables, 110
  Eggplant-Stuffed Ravioli, 113
  Italian Garden, Salad, 37
  Italian Shrimp Fettuccine, 102
  Javanese Peanut, 104
  Lobster, Richele, 100
  Penne With Vodka, 107
  Pomodoro Sauce For, 109
  Portobello, 109
  Rigatoni Carbonara, 67
  And Sausage Soup, 42
  Spinach Fettuccine With Scallops, 90
  With Swiss Chard And Smoked Gouda, 114
  Three Cheese Tortellini, 114
  Tuna Fiorintino, 94
  Vegetable Lasagna, 107

Peach
  Kimberly's, -Almond Streusel Pie, 125
  No-Bake Fresh, Pie, 124
Peanut Butter-Walnut Cookies, 150
Peas, Cauliflower Curry With Potatoes And, 110

Pecans
  Chocolate Chip-, Bread, 23
  Cinnamon, Petits, 144
  Glazed, 10
  Texas, Pie, 122
Penne With Vodka, 146.
Peppercorns, Pork Medallions With Green, Sauce 69

Peppers
  Bow Tie Pasta With Roasted Vegetables, 110
  Eggplant-Stuffed, 59
  Naples Train Station Roasted Red, 56
  And Potato Omelet, 104
  Roasted, Red & Garlic Spread, 15
  Smoked Sausage And New Potatoes With Bell, And Onions, 74
  Texas Caviar Salad, 40
Pesto Chicken Salad, 36
Pesto Toasts, 16
Petits Douces Aux Noix Et Pruneaux, 142
Pheasant With Pomegranate Sauce, 62
Pierogies, 51
Pies. See under Desserts
Pizza
  Chicken Formaggio, 81
  Rustica, 95
Poached Scallops With Curry, 91
Polenta, Sunday Chicken With Sausage And, 84
Pomegranate, Pheasant With, Sauce, 62
Pomodoro Sauce For Pasta, 109
Pork
  Artichoke And, Sauté, 67
  Citrus-Marinated, Tenderloin, 75
  With Green Olives And Tomatoes, 76
  Honey-Gingered, Tenderloin, 71
  Medallions With Green Peppercorn Sauce, 69
  Orange-Marinated, Chops, 62
  Thick, Chops On The Grill, 74
Potato(es)
  Balls, 11
  Beef 'N' Tater Bake, 78
  Cauliflower Curry With, And Peas, 110
  Crisp Rosemary, 55
  Pepper And, Omelet, 104
  Pierogies, 51
  Red Potato Salad With Chardonnay Vinaigrette, 47
  Saffron-Scented Chowder, 41
  Smoked Sausage And New, With Bell Peppers And Onions, 74
Poultry. See Chicken; Turkey
Pumpkin Cookies, 140
Pumpkin-Banana Muffins, 24

R

Raisins, Buttermilk, Pie, 116

Ralph's Waffles, 105
Raspberry, Lemon, Bars, 139
Ravioli, Eggplant-Stuffed, 113
Red Beet Chocolate Cake, 117
Red Potato Salad With Chardonnay Vinaigrette, 47
Rhubarb, Shar's, Cookies, 139
Rhubarb Bread, 27
Ribs, Sweet-Tart, 63
Rice. See also Risotto
  Black Beans And, 56
  Cheese, Loaf, 55
  South-Of-The-Border Casserole, 72
  Spanish, 54
Rigatoni Carbonara, 67
Risotto, 51
Roasted Red Pepper & Garlic Spread, 15
Rocks, 152
Romaine And Cucumber Salad With Garlic Vinaigrette, 44
Rosemary Chicken In Artichoke Sauce, 88

S

Saffron-Scented Chowder, 41
Salad(s)
  Asparagus, 32
  With Avocado Dressing, 36
  Chicken Confetti, 45
  Crunchy-Munchy Chicken, 45
  Fruit-Nut, With Curry Vinaigrette, 41
  Grilled Steak, 66
  Herbed Chicken, 48
  Italian Garden Pasta, 37
  Joanna's Signature, 44
  Mandarin Orange Nut, 40
  My Favorite Cabbage, 42
  Pesto Chicken, 36
  Red Potato, With Chardonnay Vinaigrette, 47
  Romaine And Cucumber, With Garlic Vinaigrette, 44
  Sesame Shrimp Soba, 34
  Simple, In Jicama Bowl, 37
  Strawberry & Spinach, With Poppy Seed Dressing, 48
  Texas Caviar, 40
  Tri-Color Vegetable Couscous, 46
  Tuna, 33
  Warm Cannellini Bean, 32
Salmon
  Baked, Cakes, 98

Distant And Delicious Broiled, 99
Pizza Rustica, 95
Salsa
Black Bean, 11
Melissa's, 14
Tomatillo, 16
Sandwiches, Hot Open-Faced Zucchini, 7
Santa Fe Seafood Stew, 100
Sauce(s)
Artichoke, 88
Chipotle Lime, 83
Mustard Basting, For Chicken, 88
Pomodoro, For Pasta, 109
Sausage
Easy Homemade, 53
Great Aunt Katie's, Berok, 77
Mini Quiche Cups, 12
Pasta And, Soup, 42
Seafood Gumbo, 90
Smoked, And New Potatoes With Bell
    Peppers And Onions, 74
Sunday Chicken With, And Polenta,
    84
Wonton Cups, 6
Scalloped Tomatoes, 50
Scallops
Poached, With Curry, 91
Spinach Fettuccine With, 90
Seafood Gumbo, 90
Sesame Shrimp Soba Salad, 34
Shar's Rhubarb Cookies, 139
Shrimp
Cajun Barbecue, 97
Crab And, Bisque, 44
Italian, Fettuccine, 102
Jamaican, Curry, 102
Santa Fe Seafood Stew, 100
Scampi, 99
Seafood Gumbo, 90
Sesame, Soba Salad, 34
Sicilian, 91
Spicy, William, 92
With Tasso Gravy, 92
Simple Salad In Jicama Bowl, 37
Skillet Cabbage, 50
Smoked Sausage And New Potatoes
    With Bell Peppers And Onions, 74
Soups
Bacon-Cabbage Soup, 47
Carrot, 39
Crab And Shrimp Bisque, 44

Italian Wedding, 32
Lentil Tomato, 46
Minestrone, 33
Pasta And Sausage, 42
Saffron-Scented Chowder, 41
Spinach, With Cheese Foam, 40
Squash And Roasted Corn
    Chowder, 39
Zucchini, 33
Sour Cream Carrot Cake, 124
Southern Candied Sweet Potatoes, 54
South-Of-The-Border Casserole, 72
Spanish Rice, 54
Spicy Shrimp William, 92
Spinach
Fettuccine With Scallops, 90
Frittata, 109
Fruit-Nut Salad With Curry
    Vinaigrette, 41
Greek, -Cheese Pie, 108
Italian Wedding Soup, 32
Joanna's Signature Salad, 44
Lobster Pasta Richele, 100
Soup With Cheese Foam, 40
Strawberry & , Salad With Poppy
    Seed Dressing, 48
Turkey Bundles With, 87
Squash
And Roasted Corn Chowder, 39
And Walnut Pie, 122
Steak L'Macha, 63
Strawberries
Chocolate Box Cake With, And
    Cream, 116
Chocolate-Dipped, Tart, 134
& Spinach Salad With Poppy Seed
    Dressing, 48
Summer Melon Smoothie, 6
Summertime Sun Punch, 12
Sunday Chicken With Sausage And
    Polenta, 84
Sun-Dried Tomato Dip, 10
Sweet Potatoes, Southern Candied, 54
Sweet-Tart Ribs, 63
Swiss Chard, Pasta With, And Smoked
    Gouda, 114
Swordfish, Honey-Lime Marinated, 99

T
Tangerine Tango, 11
Texas Caviar Salad, 40
Texas Pecan Pie, 122

Thick Pork Chops On The Grill, 74
Three Cheese Tortellini, 114
Tiramisu, Individual Desserts, 121
Tofu
And Broccoli Pie, 105
Fruited, Curry, 108
Tomatillo Salsa, 16
Tomatoes
Lentil, Soup, 46
Melissa's Salsa, 14
My Favorite Bruschetta, 12
Pork With Green Olives And, 76
Scalloped, 50
Sun-Dried, Dip, 10
Texas Caviar Salad, 40
Tri-Color Vegetable Couscous Salad, 46
Tropical Lime Bread, 27
Tuna Fiorentino, 94
Tuna Salad, 33
Turkey Bundle With Spinach, 87

V
Veal
Medallions Of, Trocadero, 70
Osso Buco With Gremolata, 64
Scaloppini, 71
Vegetable Lasagna, 170

W
Walnuts
Chocolate Chip-Oatmeal-, Bars, 147
Peanut Butter-, Cookies, 150
Squash And, Pie, 122
Warm Cannellini Bean Salad, 32
White Chocolate-Macadamia Nut
    Cookies, 150
Wonton Cups, 6

Z
Zucchini
Chocolate, Bread, 23
Cranberry, Bread, 29
Creamy Corn And, 60
Hot Open-Faced, Sandwiches, 7
Soup, 33
Squares, 14

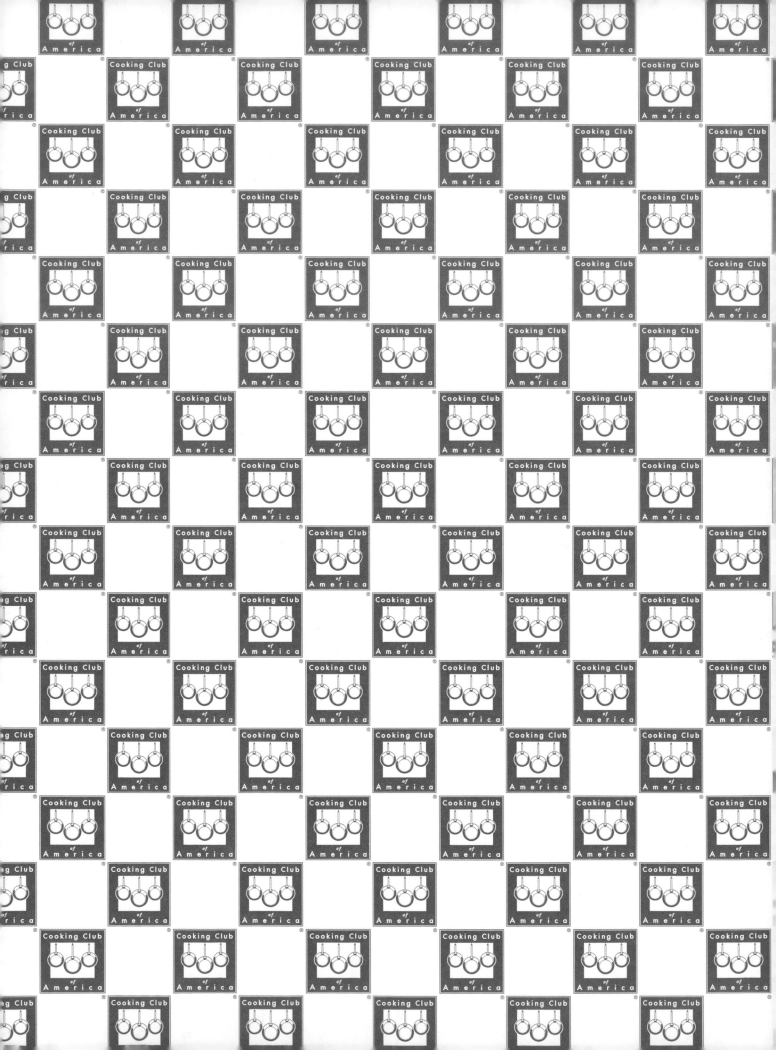